THE
INTERRACIAL
EXPERIENCE

THE INTERRACIAL EXPERIENCE

Growing Up Black/White
Racially Mixed in the United States

Ursula M. Brown

PRAEGER

Westport, Connecticut
London

Library of Congress Cataloging-in-Publication Data

Brown, Ursula M.
    The interracial experience : growing up black/white racially mixed in the United States
    / Ursula M. Brown.
        p. cm.
    Includes bibliographical references and index.
    ISBN 0–275–97046–9 (alk. paper)
        1. Racially mixed people—United States. 2. Ethnicity—United States. 3. United
    States—Race relations. I. Title.
    E184.A1B88 2001
    305.8'00973—dc21   00–039148

British Library Cataloguing in Publication Data is available.

Library of Congress Catalog Card Number: 00–039148
ISBN: 0–275–97046–9

First published in 2001

Praeger Publishers, 88 Post Road West, Westport, CT 06881
An imprint of Greenwood Publishing Group, Inc.
www.praeger.com

Printed in the United States of America

The paper used in this book complies with the
Permanent Paper Standard issued by the National
Information Standards Organization (Z39.48–1984).

10 9 8 7 6 5 4 3 2

COPYRIGHT ACKNOWLEDGMENTS

Excerpts from *Notes of a White Black Woman—Race, Color Community* (1995) by Judy Scales-Trent. Reprinted by permission of Pennsylvania State University Press.

Excerpt from "Between Two Worlds: Psychosocial Issues of Black/White Interracial Young Adults" (1997) by Ursula M. Brown in *Leading Issues in African-American Studies*, ed. Nikongo Ba Nikongo. Reprinted by permission of Carolina Academic Press.

Excerpts from "Black/White Interracial Young Adults, Quest for a Racial Identity" (January 1995) by Ursula M. Brown in the *American Journal of Orthopsychiatry*. Reprinted by permission of the *American Journal of Orthopsychiatry*. Copyright 1995 by the American Orthopsychiatry Association, Inc.

Excerpts from *List of National Interracial/Support/Advocacy Groups* by Karen Sawyer. Reprinted by permission of Karen Sawyer.

To Jim
Andrew and Roger
with Love

Contents

Acknowledgments

I would like to express my deepest appreciation to the interracial young adults who generously and courageously spoke about their experience of growing up in this country. Without their willingness to discuss their lives, struggles, frustration and joys in an open and forthright fashion, this book could not have been written. Unfortunately, pseudonyms had to be used throughout this book to protect their anonymity. However, they know who they are and I thank them wholeheartedly.

Many other persons were helpful in different ways. I am indebted to Drs. Catherine Donnell, Carol Geisler, Gladys Gonzalez, and Alice Greenwood who read selected portions of my manuscript. I want to thank them for questioning some of my unquestioned assumptions and forcing me to clarify and sharpen my findings. While their reviews led to innumerable revisions and some self-doubt, in the end their recommendations greatly improved the book. I am most grateful for the invaluable assistance of Dr. Jeanne Teresi. Her help in designing this study and data analysis enriched this book immensely. Her ability to make statistics user-friendly and her consistent and warm support throughout this project eased the difficult road of authorship. Thank you, David Palmer, Senior Production Editor at Greenwood Publishing, for giving your talent and skills in making this a better book. His critical, but tactful review of my writing has been an enlightening experience. I have drawn great strength from my mentors Drs. Phyllis Meadow, Louis Ormont, and Lena Fugeri. They were enthusiastic about this project and gave unfailing support. I also want to thank my dear friend Walli Dannich for her invaluable emotional support during the years I was immersed in the interracial world and Bill Dannich for his rescue missions during my various computer crises. I am also deeply indebted to the many people who were instrumental in finding candidates for this study. Among them were the Bolden family, Janet Warner, Gale Monaco, Jessie Campell and the students of various universities. I extend my deepest gratitude for their support, as without people like them this study would not have been possible.

Special thanks to my mother, Gusti Eder, whose support and love has been truly unconditional, and my father, Anton Zell, who did not always agree with my path in life, but graciously accepted my diversions. My sister, Angelika Zell has been there for me at important times. She is very special to me and I deeply regret that she lives so far away. I am indebted to the Widmer family whose steady presence, warmth, generosity, and interest have sustained me through life and writing this book. Thank you for being there, dear Elfi and Gunther!

The inspiration to writing this book came originally from my two interracial sons, Andrew and Roger. Their struggle and ultimate success in finding a racial home in both the black and white world has deeply touched and impressed me. They have been wonderful sons whose love, care, honesty and genuine interest in this project has been a precious gift. Andrew initially introduced me to a circle of interracial people who helped get this project off the ground. Roger followed suit. Their sensitive but critical reading of each chapter improved the quality of this book greatly. Thank you for your time, wisdom and incredible support!

Finally, I want to thank my husband Dr. James Brown who was my best friend and soul mate. He died after a long and heroic battle with cancer while I was in the final writing phase of this book. His love, generosity and compassion for people influenced my life and work deeply. Without his confidence in me, I might never have tried writing this book. His unceasing patience, understanding, love and support provided me with the emotional sustenance vital to conducting this study. Thank you, dearest Jim! You are greatly missed and you will always be in my heart.

CHAPTER 1

Introduction: Three Interracial People

Throughout the history of the United States, children of black/white interracial couples have struggled with acceptance and racial group membership questions. Whites[1] have discriminated against them because of their blackness and because they represent the violation of an emotion-laden taboo against racial mixing. In turn, blacks envied them for the privileges they enjoyed in a white-dominated society, yet also resented them for their snobbish attitudes and treated them with suspicion in terms of racial group loyalties.

The negative impact of these attitudes was compounded by a peculiar system of racial classification. With such brief, marginally important exceptions as the small mulatto castes in some antebellum southern cities, anybody with black ancestry or visible signs of black roots was considered black in this country. Incorporating both blackness and whiteness in one body and one self, this mandate denied interracial[2] people whiteness, rendered their racial existence invisible, and pressured them to restrict racial identification to their black parent. As a result, the integration of partial identifications into a unified identity configuration, which according to Erik Erikson (1959) is the hallmark of healthy identity development, was undermined. Finally, surrendering whiteness in favor of blackness in a society where blackness is associated with negative stereotypes, discrimination, and oppression becomes extremely difficult.

Thus interracial children have to negotiate all the developmental challenges that confront uniracial children. In addition, they have to face a unique set of emotional hurdles. These stem from their mixed racial background, a world that has deprived them of the right to define themselves as who they are, and communities that may resent them for their blackness, interracialness, or whiteness.

THE YEAR 2000

In the mid-1980s a burgeoning of interracial family organizations and literature occurred. Interracial families became increasingly demanding of a socially and institutionally recognized category that allowed their children to accurately define themselves.

In 1993, the Office of Management and Budget (OMB) held hearings to determine whether a multiracial category should be part of the census in the year 2000. The demand for such a category was voted down with the explanation that not enough information about the issue existed. However, a few years later under renewed pressure, the OMB resumed the debate. A multiracial classification, which had originally been considered, was rejected since it only indicated the presence of a mixed race background, but little else. Instead, the OMB issued the rule that people be allowed to express their multiracial heritage in whatever way they see themselves. President Clinton adopted the new rules on Oct. 29, 1997 (Holmes, 1997). For the first time, people are allowed to identify themselves on federal forms as a member of more than one race. The reception of this ruling by the public has been mixed, for the "one drop of black blood" rule has been deeply ingrained into American consciousness and passionately upheld for centuries. How long it will take the American public to change its mind about who is black, white, or mixed remains to be seen. It seems unlikely that a major transformation will occur quickly, for a change in the present system of racial classification will challenge one of the most psychologically and socially sensitive rules upon which the American social hierarchy has rested. A revamping of federal data will have broad implications not only for the tabulation of the census but also for the political and economic power structure of America (Barr and Fletcher, 1997).

For black/white interracial children, this reluctance will translate into continuous pressure to deny the white part of themselves; for the parents, a continuation of bewilderment of how to deal with the question of their children's racial group membership. Trying to fit into the socially prescribed racial mold that can only accommodate half of who the interracial child is seems to be an enormous struggle. For first-generation racially mixed people, the freedom to embrace openly and publicly both parts of their racial heritage promises to be the most important step in smoothing their path toward a clear racial identity and healthy self-esteem.

Unfortunately, in a society that has traditionally used racial classification to legitimize social inequalities and oppression, the psychological benefits associated with the freedom to identify oneself as a member of more than one race may be seriously compromised. The splintering of black and interracial groups into separate entities will decrease the size of each. This may jeopardize their already precarious political and socioeconomic position and undermine their ability to obtain social and economic justice. How to reconcile these conflicting psychological and sociological needs is a challenge for interracial people as well as for social scientists. This challenge cannot be addressed in a meaningful manner without understanding more fully the impact that our present system has on the psychosocial adjustment of mixed-race people. The lack of empirical research has handicapped this understanding as well as our ability to provide meaningful support to this group. This book is intended to address the gap.

A journey into the world of three interracial people will offer the reader a glimpse into the lives, struggles, frustrations, and joys of biracial people. Psychosocial issues that are unique to them will be highlighted. In addition, experiences that influenced their adjustment will be addressed. Their accounts will demonstrate that the path toward a racial identity in mixed-race people does not necessarily lead to blackness, as is commonly assumed, but may defy social convention. The three interracial people presented here do not represent all black/white interracial people. Rather, their dilemmas and their resolutions constitute key patterns that were repeated in the lives of the 119 people I interviewed while researching this book.

MATTHEW: TOWARD A BLACK IDENTITY

Matthew[3] was twenty-two years old when I met him. He had just graduated from college and had returned to New York City where he grew up and wanted to settle. Matthew had a medium-brown complexion, and despite having facial features and curly hair suggesting white roots, he embraced a strong black identity. Over the phone he had asked to meet me at his favorite downtown jazz club. My concerns about acoustical problems were alleviated as we entered the club and were met by the beautiful and mellow sounds of a jazz quartet. In addition, Matthew had requested a balcony seat so that we could talk comfortably. Over a hearty evening meal, Matthew shared his experiences of growing up with a white mother and a black father.

When Matthew was young, he thought he was adopted because he looked so different than his mother did. She was able not only to dispel his doubts but also to encourage him not to "limit himself to one race" and to embrace both sides of his racial heritage.

His father, a jazz musician, took a different approach. He wanted Matthew to "come to grips" with the reality that the outside world would view him as black. To accomplish this goal, he made black culture and particularly jazz an intricate part of Matthew's life. He also sent Matthew to a predominately black elementary school where the principal, a black nationalist, made sure that his students became acquainted with black history, black traditions, and the "Black Power" and "Black Pride" principles. Matthew developed a strong black identity in this environment, and he liked his teachers—particularly the principal, who became an important role model for him.

However, his sense of well-being and belonging in this mostly black social milieu became disturbed when he was seen with his white mother. Being connected to her made him stand out as different, raised questions about his authenticity as a black person, and made him vulnerable to shaming, taunts, and caustic remarks. At the same time he worried about hurting his mother's feelings and losing her love if she knew about his fears, his feelings of shame, and his wishes to hide her.

The change to a mostly all-white high school brought relief to the conflicts he experienced about his mother. However, his blackness became a source of frustration and turmoil for it presented a barrier to acceptance. The message that "black is beautiful," prominent in the black elementary school he attended, was changed to blackness is inferior and you should "act white." Upset and angry about the school's prejudices and assimilation attempts, he became increasingly defiant, and as he explained, he emerged from high school a "pretty intense Black Nationalist."

Exposure to different political, historical, and cultural viewpoints in college seemed to diminish his anger toward whites. His outlook on race and racial issues began to broaden. He dated both black and white women and did not rule out interracial marriage, but his strong black identity remained intact. He explained, "No matter who I marry, I will be who I am. If it's black, I will be black. If it's white, I still would be black. In every way shape or form, I will be black." Matthew seemed at peace with who he was. His black identity was in harmony with his inner self, his physical characteristics as well as social stipulations. The identification with his black father, his phenotype, and his socialization in a predominately black social milieu laid the foundation for a strong black identity in adulthood.

SIDNEY: TRYING TO FIT IN

Sidney, a petite young woman with olive-toned skin, light-brown curly hair, and the facial features of a black person, was twenty-four years old when I met her. An interracial woman I had interviewed for the purpose of this study introduced us. Sidney felt that interracial people are the "forgotten" people in this country and was pleased about the study and the prospect of participating in it. We met for the interview in a neighborhood cafe in Boston, where she had been working part time in the computer field.

Sidney arrived at the appointed place a few minutes late. After screening the cafe, she steered toward me, apologized for her lateness, and settled down. Over pastry and coffee she began talking about a rather sad and lonely life that had been shaped and dominated by racism. When she was born, her white grandparents in the South disowned her mother and told friends and relatives that their daughter had died. Sidney's mother was devastated by her parents' reaction. Her pleadings to change their minds seemed to fall on deaf ears. Only after she broke off with Sidney's father and married a white man did the rift begin to mend.

Sidney felt accepted by her stepfather, a blue-collar worker who eventually adopted her. The relationship with her mother, however, deteriorated over the years because of the mother's obvious preference for a fair-skinned half brother and sister. Whether this preference was due to some personality traits of Sidney, racial bigotry the mother had internalized within a racist society, or the mother's difficulties in coping with the societal devaluation she suffered for having a racially mixed child is not evident from Sidney's account. What is clear is that the mother was uncomfortable with her daughter's black roots. Sidney recalled, "My mother did not accept me as who I was. She wanted me to be white. I was 'good' when I 'acted white,' and 'bad' when I 'acted black.' " She interpreted her mother's communication as "black is lesser than white, black is negative, and being black is unacceptable."

Sidney did not know whether her biological father was dead or alive. Her mother rarely spoke of him and then mostly in derogatory terms. No efforts were made to establish contact with other black relatives or friends or to acquaint her with black culture. In a predominately white neighborhood and school, she was subjected to teasing and racial slurs pertaining to blacks or racially mixed children. Not being exposed to interracial or black role models with whom she could identify and who could counteract the negative messages she was getting about blackness, Sidney felt little connection to blacks. Her own blackness was a source of discomfort and shame. She remembered, "My association to black people was people on welfare, dark-skinned rapists, uneducated. I did not know that there were educated blacks, so I certainly did not see being black as a positive thing."

Sidney felt tormented by conflicts and confusion about who she was racially. She wanted to be white, blend in, and feel part of her family and her white neighborhood. During her adolescent years, she became increasingly withdrawn and depressed. Her sense of being different was exacerbated when her friends began dating and she failed to be asked out throughout her high school years. Attributing her lack of suitors to her own personal deficits she recalled, "I felt very ugly and I thought that there was something deeply wrong with me." She could not wait to leave home and a community where she felt out of place, unwanted, and shamed for her blackness.

College marked the beginning of a better life. She started dating, made some friends, and began to come to grips with the fact that she would never be able to pass as white. With the acceptance of this reality, she became more interested in her black roots. For a short time, she joined the black college community. However, her hopes of finding a social, intellectual, and emotional home there failed. Her unwillingness to deny her whiteness and her white cultural orientation presented a barrier to acceptance. Finally, the racial tensions between black and white college communities made membership in both an impossible challenge. She remembered, "I really tried very hard to fit in, but the black professors saw whites as the enemy and here I had white friends and this whole white family. Also, the campus was very segregated. I would try to be friends with the black kids, but to be friends with them, you could not be friends with the white kids. It was definitely an either/or." Looking for a "safer means" to become acquainted with the black side of herself, she turned to books. While her reading seemed to help her to become less biased, her identification with blacks and pride in her own blackness failed to flourish.

After Sidney graduated from college, her energies continued to be directed at becoming comfortable with herself. Ties with her family had been severed with the exception of one sister. "She is my family," Sidney explained sadly and defiantly. Her family's and community's inability to embrace her as who she was left her angry, bitter, and deeply hurt.

CLAUDETTE: OUT OF THE CLOSET

Claudette, a twenty-five-year-old college graduate with light brown skin, curly dark brown hair, and expressive eyes was in the midst of preparing her wedding to a European immigrant when I first met her. She had just moved into a new apartment and had changed her job to work in an art gallery. While she seemed consumed with the changes in her life, she readily agreed to an interview when she heard the name of the family friend who had recommended that I call her. She invited me to come to her apartment, which, as she laughingly explained, was not furnished yet but had a table and chairs "enough to hold a good conversation."

Claudette greeted me graciously at the door. After inviting me into the living room and wondering if I would join her for a light supper, she served an attractively decorated platter of smoked fish, cheeses, fresh bread, and fruits. The table setting, fresh flowers, and candles and Claudette's casual but tasteful clothing suggested her sense of style. During our meal, Claudette told me about her coming wedding. The fact that she was crossing racial and cultural boundaries with her choice of mate seemed of little significance to her. Her white Jewish father and black Christian mother had married before mixed-race marriages were legalized in 1967 and apparently had weathered successfully the various storms that confronted interracial couples at that time. Things had improved since then, Claudette felt, for interracial marriages are more common, less of a novelty, and therefore more accepted. What concerned her more, she explained, was that her children would not have to go through the identity problems she had encountered. She was pleased that interracial families were beginning to organize and fight for a socially and legally recognized interracial category, which she felt would have spared her and many others like her much anguish.

Claudette remembered considerable uncertainty about who she was while growing up. Her interracial self-perceptions, which her parents seemed to foster, had changed during grade school to a mostly white identity. She was not quite sure how this happened for she attended a private elementary school that prided itself on embracing cultural diversity. Her parents, both successful professionals, tried to instill pride in both racial heritages, by exposing her to Jewish and Christian traditions. Holidays of both sides were celebrated, and both black and white relatives were an integral part of Claudette's upbringing.

Despite her family's efforts, the message that white is better than black, which continues to be prevalent in this white-dominated country, seemed to increasingly affect her. In an effort to undo what she perceived as a blemish, she overcompensated with high achievements in school and as a ballet dancer. She recalled: "I was very compulsive about everything, a perfectionist and an overachiever. I wanted to be the best. I drove myself awfully hard."

It was not until her adolescence that she came to terms with the fact that she was not white. The identification with her black mother, greater emotional readiness to own both parts of her racial makeup, as well as her phenotype, which clearly showed signs of her black heritage, seemed to play an important role in her acceptance of that reality. With the resolution of her racial group membership question, Claudette began to feel more comfortable with herself and looked forward to becoming more deeply acquainted with her black roots in college. However, the racial tensions there destroyed that dream. She remembered: "Blacks sat in their little corner in the dining room and whites in theirs. It was really strange." When she declined an invitation to become a member of the Black Student Organization, refused to give up her white friends, and insisted on the recognition of her dual racial background, she started to attract negative attention within the black community. The situation deteriorated further when she failed to take the black side in a racial controversy that was debated in the student newspaper. Being viewed as a traitor in the black community made life increasingly unbearable for her. She recalled being screamed at, taunted, ridiculed, and threatened with physical violence by a few militant black students. Frightened to attend classes and eat in the dining hall, she started to withdraw to the safety of her room.

After her freshman year, Claudette transferred to a college that was more receptive to racial differences. Much happier there, she completed her college education. Growing up as an interracial person in America, however, left a bitter taste in her mouth. At the end of the interview she confided: "If I had a choice, I would live in a foreign country, probably Europe or South America. My experience has been that people celebrate racial differences in these countries, while they are condemned in America."

A CLOSER LOOK AT THREE LIVES

These three accounts demonstrate the crucial role of experiential, physical, demographic, and personal factors in the psychosocial adjustment of interracial people. In a culture that idealizes whiteness and devalues blackness, black children frequently identify with the white dominant race (Brody, 1963; Erikson, 1959; Clark and Clark, 1939 and 1947; Cross, 1971; Greenwald and Oppenheimer, 1968; Moreland, 1966; Powell-Hopson, 1985; Tatum, 1997). With the interracial person being half white and therefore closer to a white Euro-American frame of reference and privileges than uniracial blacks, becoming black is even more of a challenge. The family, school, and community can play a vital role in mastering this challenge.

Matthew's identity conflicts stemmed from not being black enough rather than wanting to be white. The child of a racially mixed marriage, he represented a betrayal to the "black cause" in the mostly black social milieu in which he grew up. Therefore, his whiteness became a liability and a source of shame that was reinforced by the presence of his mother. The close relationship he enjoyed with her in the privacy of their home was contaminated as a result.

The exploration of the question of who am I, which is part of healthy adolescent development, was undercut by fears that the white high school he attended would "stamp out his blackness." While immersion in the black world protected him from identity diffusion, rejecting his whiteness undermined the integration of his black and white identity parts into a consolidated gestalt. However, embracing an identity that was in harmony with the way he looked and was socially sanctioned seemed to outweigh the cost of that. While education and greater emotional maturity broadened his view on race, he continued to view himself as black. Only once during the almost three-hour interview did he acknowledge the reality of his biracial background.

When the message that black is bad is part of a family and community legacy, the resistance to embrace blackness intensifies. Sidney demonstrates this problem. Lacking contact with black role models, she was unable to counteract the constant denigration of her color. As a result, Sidney experienced her black roots as alien, humiliating, and shameful. Because she was surrounded by whites, developing a white identity was inevitable and so were the conflicts associated with an identity that is considered fraudulent under the "one drop" rule. Moreover, the white identity clashed with her physical appearance and society's view of her. Experiencing herself as a white person in a black body, her sense of self was painfully distorted. She longed for a resolution of the conflicts created by the discrepant psychic and physical realities. Becoming black seemed to promise relief from her suffering. However, the ongoing antagonism between blacks and whites in this country, which was presented as a microcosm in the college community, prevented her from forging ties with blacks. Having to rely on books to learn about her black heritage kept her sense of blackness or interracialness on a fragile footing. The wish to be white and her inability to do so continued to haunt her in young adulthood.

Claudette, similarly to Sidney, thought of herself as white when she was a child. Unlike Sidney's family, however, Claudette's embraced an interracial life style and worked hard to counteract the negative societal messages regarding blackness. Despite her family's efforts, however, Claudette identified with the white majority culture and a white beauty ideal that was particularly prominent and celebrated in the world of ballet. Unable to cope with the reality of being different and less valued than her peers, she seemed in denial that her light brown skin clashed with her white racial self-perception and precluded passing as white. As she was approaching adolescence and her physical darkness invited consistently discrepant internal and external messages regarding her race, her denial began to diminish. The identity transformation that occurred at that time was associated with considerable turmoil. However, as her identification with her black mother and other black role models became more comfortable and the messages of pride in both racial backgrounds inherent in her family as well as her racially diverse neighborhood began to bear fruit, her interracial self-perception became stronger. She came to grips with the reality that she was not white, and began to embrace her mother's assurance that being biracial made her special and could enrich her life. With the consolidation of black and white identity parts into a unified identity gestalt, her sense of self improved and she enjoyed the inner peace associated with having found a racial home that reflected who she was.

While Claudette had struggled with identity question throughout her childhood and adolescence, she did not enter a crisis state until she went to college and her interracial self-perceptions and white cultural orientation and friendships with whites came under attack. Claudette's coping skills seemed insufficient to master such pressures. Her flight into a safer college environment eventually allowed her to refocus on her education.

RACIAL IDENTITY IN PERSPECTIVE

In a white-dominated society where racial group membership continues to determine access to social, psychological, and economic privileges, race plays an important part in people's lives. The importance of racial identity in the development of the self is stressed by Cookie White Stephan (1992). She explains, "Ethnic identity, the identification of an individual or group of individuals with a particular ethnic group or groups, is particularly important to the self because it is a master status, an identity that overrides all others' judgments of the self. As such, it is also basic to the establishment of self-meaning" (p. 51).

One of the purposes of this book is to explore the ways black/white interracial people negotiate their quest of a racial identity and self-esteem in a society that recognizes only half of who they are. I will also take an in-depth look at family, community, school, college, and the dating arena to see what kind of experiences enhance or undermine their journey. Their struggle for acceptance in both the black and white world and the impact on racial self-perceptions and self-esteem will be examined. Some adaptive measures in coping with their social anonymity and racist attitudes against them will be highlighted. Finally, I will discuss strategies of families, mental health professionals, and society that could provide meaningful support to the interracial child. However, before addressing these topics I will consider issues concerning the study itself and then such broader concerns as the role of color in our society and the historical forces that shape present attitudes toward mixed-race people.

NOTES

1. The terms white and black are used to refer to individuals who are the offspring of two socially defined white (European-American) or two socially defined black (African-American) parents. There are no pure races left anywhere in the world.

2. The term interracial refers to the biological child of one socially defined black and one socially defined white parent. This word is also used to refer to marriages (and other conjugal relationships) between a black person and a white person.

3. To protect the identity of study participants, all names and places of residence are fictitious.

CHAPTER 2

An Orientation of the Study

HISTORICAL PERSPECTIVE: MULATTOS DURING SLAVERY AND BEYOND

Society at Large

During the Colonial period in America, blacks were considered inferior, even subhuman. This belief assured profit for the slave masters and to some degree conformed to religious ethics. Therefore, the rationale that made slavery acceptable was straightforward and offered peace of mind: If blacks were not really human beings, they did not have to be treated as such.

The nonhuman status of slaves, however, did not stop white slave masters from engaging in sexual relationships with their female slaves. The small number of European women in the thinly populated agricultural areas of the Colonial South created a climate in which not only sexual but emotional bonds between slave master and their black female slaves existed. These attachments were frequently extended to the offspring of such relationships. Thus the mulattos of the deep South typically came from upper-class men (Lebsock, 1990).

Unfortunately, mulatto children were also the product of rape. Embedded in plantation life was the raping of enslaved black women by their masters or the master's sons, by overseers and by neighbors (Huggins, 1990). While in the antebellum American South, a black man faced lynching at the mere suggestion that he had touched a white woman, it was not a crime for a white man to force a black woman to have sexual intercourse under most jurisdictions. Lawmakers typically portrayed female Negroes as promiscuous or wanton "Jezebels." Because of their presumed licentiousness and their lack of maternal instincts, the legal system often deprived them of the right to marry or to get custody of their children. Similar reasons were used to deny them legal protection from rape. A state court in Mississippi (*State vs. George*, 37 Miss. 316, 317), ruled in 1859: "The regulation of law, as to the white race, on the subject of sexual intercourse, do not and cannot, for obvious reasons, apply to slaves; their intercourse is promiscuous, and the violation of a female slave by a male slave would be a mere assault and battery." White men were rarely convicted for raping black women. However, prosecution of whites for fornication, cohabitation and seduction were fairly common (Fisher, 1993).

In the upper South, racial mixing also occurred between slaves from Africa and indentured servants from Europe. Both groups were used by large landowners to help clear the land and plant crops (Williams, 1980). Working side by side and sharing the same type of life, slaves and the indentured servants not only bonded as friends but sometimes became lovers and had children.

Not all mulattos, however, were subjected to slavery during Colonial times. Some enjoyed their freedom because they were the offspring of free colored parents, had free colored mothers and slave fathers, or in some instances were the children of white females and black slave fathers (Frazier, 1957).

African women had a profound impact on white men. Trapped in the repressive norms of Christian ethics, which equated sex with sin, white men seemed to long for black women who were supposedly animalistic in nature. Some white men had formed early emotional attachments to black women who had nursed them as infants and helped raise them as children. With premarital sex a powerfully imposed taboo for white women, the white man's first sexual experience frequently occurred with a black woman (Huggins, 1990). Also, some pretty mulatto women became the concubines of wealthy white gentlemen. These young women, called "fancy girls," were frequently auctioned off at "quadroon balls" in New Orleans and Charleston (Davis, 1991). Some of these concubines were resold after their owners got tired of them, while some were kept for a lifetime.

In general the threat of racial mixing has plagued the American psyche since Europeans began enslaving Africans and exporting them to the American colonies. Most white Americans simply did not want people of color mixing with them. What people of color did among themselves mattered little to them, because it did not threaten the boundary between white and nonwhite. Also, whites understood that if sexual unions between Negroes and whites were tolerated, ethical questions regarding slavery would soon arise. The first public record of sexual relations between a white man and a Negro woman was entered in 1630 in Virginia. It read: "September 17, 1630, Hugh Davis is to be soundly whipped before an assembly of Negroes and others for abusing himself to the dishonor of God and the shame of Christians by defiling his body in lying with a Negro" (Lythcott-Haimes, p. 534). As early as 1661, the first miscegenation laws were recorded in Maryland. Legislators proclaimed that fornication between whites and Negroes was equivalent to bestiality. Eventually thirty-eight states adopted anti-miscegenation laws. However, the masses—whites and nonwhites—failed to adhere to these statutes. Sexual, romantic, and marital (usually not legal) relationships continued as before between Negroes and whites.

With the steady increase in the number of mulatto children and with these children on the outside of the existing social order, it become necessary to establish their legal status. For example, the right to own property, run for office, and vote was reserved for whites and denied to blacks. Were these mixed-race children to enjoy the free status of their white parent or assume the slave status of their black parent? Therefore the resolution of the question regarding their racial classification became paramount. The colonial lawmakers found a solution that worked to their benefit. In 1662, deviating from traditional English law that held that children assume the status of their fathers, the Virginia legislature ruled that mulatto children should have the status of their mothers. Since most of the mothers were black, this law assured that racially mixed people could not claim the freedom their white fathers enjoyed. It also permitted the white masters to preserve the economic and social status quo and gave them unfettered ability to increase the slave population through sexual transgressions. Almost every state in the antebellum South devised elaborate systems of racial classifications. The following example demonstrates these race-defining statutes (Williamson, 1980):

Fraction of "Black Blood" = "Race"

0	white
⅛	octoroon
¼	quadroon
½	mulatto
¾	griffe
⅞	sacatra
1	Negro

Under this scheme, anyone with at least one-eighth "black blood" was considered black. Underlying these statutes was a belief that race is biological. The eighteenth-century Swedish botanist and taxonomist Carolus Linnaeus had promoted this notion. He devised a system of classifications of all living things. (Human being are all members of the kingdom *Animalia*, the phylum *Chordata*, the class *Mamalia*, the order *Primates*, the family *Homididea*, the genus *Homo*, and the species *Homo Sapiens*.) In the nineteenth century the founder of scientific anthropology, Johann Friedrich Blumenbach, expanded Linnaeus's scheme to include human races on the basis of geography and observed physical differences. The famous naturalists of the nineteenth century—George Cuvier, Charles Lyell, and Charles Darwin—the intellectual descendants of Linneaus and Blumenbach, promoted the typological view of races in which people are arranged hierarchically. Caucasians in this hierarchy were found on top and Africans at the bottom—in terms of physical ability and moral qualities.

Mulattos held a higher position than blacks in this hierarchy because of their white blood. They enjoyed psychological and social privileges that were denied to uniracial blacks. They were viewed as more intelligent and capable than blacks and were frequently spared from the backbreaking labor of field hands. Instead they often worked in the "big house" and benefited from various degrees of education. The positive regard that these children often experienced from their white fathers was sometimes translated into their being freed from the shackles of slavery and established in business, trade, or farming (Frazier, 1957). The privileges enjoyed by mixed-race people frequently aroused envy and jealousy in the black community and ultimately caused dissension between the two groups.

The distinction that was made between mulattos and blacks by no means assured acceptance of the "mixed bloods" by the white community. Whites believed that the addition of white blood elevated the blackness of mixed-race children. However, because of their black blood, mulattos could never attain the skills and intellectual competency of the white race. In general, whites were uncomfortable with mulattos. To them mulattos represented either a "reminder of slavery, of the defilement of Negro women, of fathers who were masters and of brothers who were also servants" (Berzon, 1974, p. 6707). Negative stereotypes of racially mixed people were popularized in the nineteenth century by scientists, academics, sociologists, judges, members of the clergy, and lay people. The genetically, mentally, morally inferior, and maladjusted mulatto character began to be engraved in the American psyche.

Sexual relations between blacks and whites diminished with the mounting tensions about slavery between South and North and the advent of the Civil War. The social and economic devastation that resulted from the Civil War and vigilante groups like the Ku Klux Klan that had formed during this time were instrumental in keeping the races apart (Davis, 1991). Nevertheless, two hundred years of racial mixing had left their mark and produced a rainbow of skin colors.

To preserve their status after the Civil War, mulattos began to actively discriminate against darker-skinned blacks by segregating themselves in separate communities. Elite social clubs were created by mulattos such as the Bon Ton Society in Washington, D.C., and the Blue Vein Society of Nashville. Since social privileges were associated with lighter skin, admission to these clubs was based on skin color. The potential member had to be light enough for the bluish veins on the wrist to be visible (Frazier, 1962). Not until after the Black Renaissance of the 1920s did the influence and prevalence of the mulatto social clubs weaken, although prejudice about skin color and class continues to exist. Remnants of the snobbish attitudes are found in today's elite black social clubs. For example, clubs like Jack and Jill and the Links have a majority of light-skinned members (Williams, 1981). Ironically, first-generation interracial children are sometimes discriminated against and barred from membership in these clubs. They represent a betrayal of the black cause, which frowns on racial mixing.

The system of racial classification that categorizes a person with any black ancestry as black remained unaltered by the civil rights laws of the 1960s. The Louisiana legislature in 1970 saw it necessary to distinguish precisely between who is white and who is black:

In signifying race, person having one-thirty second or less of Negro blood shall be deemed, described or designated by any public official in the state of Louisiana as "colored," a "mulatto," a "black," a "Negro," a "griffe," an "Afro-

American," a "quadroon," a "mestizo," a "colored person" or a "person of color."
(Louisiana Act 46 enacted in 1970 and codified in § 42:267 of the Louisiana re-
vised statute annotated, and repeated in 1983 by section 1 of Louisiana Act 441.)

With one-thirty-second "black blood" being the equivalent of one
great-great-great-grandparent, and people rarely knowing their ancestors
more than a few generations back, one must assume that quite a few
people regarded themselves as white, when in actuality they should have
viewed and defined themselves as black. Thus many Americans may
have wittingly or unwittingly violated racial status laws. It is estimated
that 30 to 70 percent of African Americans have white relatives in their
ancestral history and that a significant proportion of white-identified
people have a multiracial background (Root, 1992).

Not until 1983 was the Louisiana statute amended. By that time every
state had abandoned racial classification on the basis of fractional per-
centage of blackness. Derogatory terms like "octoroon" and "Sambo"
had disappeared. However, the officially codified system that was prevalent from the era of slavery into the twentieth century was replaced by
an unofficial reliance on the "one drop of black blood" rule (Lythcott-
Haimes, 1994). This rule holds that anyone with the smallest trace of
African background is black. Consequently, a person still has to be *all*
white in the United States to be considered white, while a person with
any black blood is still black. The central premise of this mandate is
blatantly racist. It implies that black blood is contaminated, while white
blood is pure or that the former is not on a par with the latter (Spickard,
1989). While no other country in the New World with the exception of
Canada defines people racially by a measurable amount of black blood
(Degler, 1986), this notion is so ingrained in the American psyche that
neither blacks nor whites give it much thought. In fact, many interracial
people joined blacks in the 1960s Black Power movement.

Learning to take pride in their blackness was of immense psychological importance to interracial people. For they, like many blacks, had
incorporated the societal devaluation of blackness and idealization of
whiteness. Consequently, the message that "black is beautiful" was a
most positive one for the collective psyche of black and interracial people. What was less beneficial about the movement was the message that
they were not black enough and the taunting, shaming, or rejection that
occurred for having a white parent.

The Civil Rights movement of the 1960s and the 1967 Supreme Court
decision, *Loving v. Virginia*, which abolished miscegenation laws, opened

Table 1

Black/White Interracial Marriage: 1970 and 1998

Interracial Married Couples	1998	1970
Black/white	330,000	65,000
Black husband/White wife	210,000	41,000
White husband/Black wife	120,000	24,000

Source of data: U.S. Bureau of the Census, Current Population Reports.

the door to interracial marriages and an interracial baby boom. As Table 1 demonstrates, in 1970 the U.S. Bureau of the Census counted 65,000 black/white interracial marriages. This number increased to 330,000 in 1998, a rise of 507 percent in twenty-eight years.

The type of interracial marriage remained relatively stable over the years. The black husband/white wife marital pattern continues to be the most frequent one. The exact number of children that these unions have produced is not known, since interracial children are classified as black and not all black/white couples with children are married.

The 2000 census will mark the end of the official anonymity of interracial or multiracial children. However, not only may the public be resistant to changing their minds about who is black, but interracial people may be hesitant to make public an identity that has not been recognized by whites and, until now, was certain to invite rejection from the one place interracial people could call home—the black community. Past attempts to obtain recognition for their dual racial heritage have resulted in angry accusations by blacks that they wanted to distance themselves from their blackness. Dr. Robert B. Hill, director of the institute for Urban Research at the Morgan State University and chairman of the bureau's Advisory Committee on the African Research Population, said, "We think people who have been pushing this [multiracial category] want somehow to de-emphasize the racial component, the black component. We are convinced of that. They say they are multiracial, which means I am less black or somehow I can have a way of not having to check myself as black" (Holmes, 1996, p. A 25).

The sociological as well as the psychological consequences of the proposed change are yet to be seen. Whether these changes will unify or further separate this country along color lines will have to be carefully monitored by social scientists.

Mental Health Community

In the advent of the interracial baby boom, several mental health professionals for the first time began to examine formally the psychosocial adjustment of interracial children and the effect of the negative stereotypes that had been held for most of America's history. The information they gathered (Adams, 1973; Gibbs, 1987; Piskacek and Golub, 1973; Teicher, 1968) came primarily from patients in mental health settings. Not surprisingly, a portrait of an emotionally troubled and ill-adjusted marginal person began to reemerge. But when several social scientists in the 1970s began to study interracial children in nonclinical settings, this image was challenged. For example, one study showed (Spivey, 1984) that the ambivalent feelings about racial identity that he observed in interracial adolescents did not prevent them from enjoying above-average levels of self-esteem and average or above-average psychosocial adjustment. Moreover, they were high achievers and coped successfully with a variety of social and educational challenges. Similarly, Arnold (1984) found that interracial children might be ambivalent over which race to identify with but that their self-concept did not differ from the general population. While these researchers lacked consensus about the emotional well-being of interracial children, they all seemed to agree that in a society where race is omnipresent, having the means to define oneself as who one is becomes crucial to a clear racial identity.

WHO IS THE RESEARCHER? WHO ARE THE PEOPLE TO BE STUDIED AND WHAT ARE THE METHODS?

Researcher

My interest in interracial people originates from two experiences. The first and most important one, perhaps, is being the white partner in a racially mixed marriage and having raised two interracial children. In the process of parenting my children, it became quite apparent to me that for their psychosocial adjustment and self-esteem, meeting the love and nurturing needs they had in common with all children was not enough. Their interracial heritage created unique challenges.

My understanding of my children's experiences was handicapped by two factors. First, my European background rendered me relatively unfamiliar with American racial tension. Second, due to my own racially homogeneous background, I had never walked in the shoes of an interracial child. Consequently, my understanding of the special needs of my own children had to be gained by observation, discussion, and guess-work. My children were good teachers, but I would have welcomed some external support system or professional or literary guidance that focused on the experiences and the special needs of mixed-race children. Since these were virtually nonexistent, creating an environment that would foster a healthy identity frequently became a matter of trial and error.

Although both of my sons are presently successful young professionals and have succeeded in the quest of a healthy racial identity, my own experience and my knowledge of the frustrations of other interracial couples who are compelled to raise their children in a virtual vacuum of external support systems represented a major motivating force in conducting this study.

The second stimulus for my choice of topic relates to my professional orientation. Having worked for several years with socio-economically deprived families and individuals, I have become convinced of the crucial and intimate relationship between mental health and environmental forces. This relationship seemed to be particularly intense for interracial children who grow up in a society that continues to devalue children of color and stipulate that they deny their whiteness. Also, as a mental health professional treating interracial children and their families, I have seen interracial people on all levels of the adjustment spectrum. This impression of complexity has been strengthened not only by my own experience of raising two interracial children but also by my membership in an Interracial Family Alliance. It seemed to me that the ability of interracial people to cope with the complex and often bewildering challenge of growing up biracial in the United States was related to particular experiences within the family, community, schools, and the dating arena. Also, their racial appearance as well as personal idiosyncrasy derived from the interactional genetic and experiental factors seems to play a role in their adjustment. Consequently, when I set out to formally study the problems confronting interracial children and the solutions they might have developed in their struggles, I focused on these areas.

Methodology

To accomplish this goal, I wanted to study interracial young adults rather than children to gain understanding as to what kind of experiences and physical and demographic factors had enhanced their ability to resolve the question Who am I? Identity consolidation should more or less have taken place at the end of adolescence. As Eric Erikson (1959) noted, turning eighteen marks the end of adolescence and the beginning of adulthood. In general, at this developmental juncture, ego identity has been tentatively defined and one begins to experience an inner sense of sameness and continuity that is complemented by the sameness and continuity of what one means to others. I also wanted to see what kind of factors influenced their overall adjustment, especially their self-esteem and conflicts about racial group membership.

To produce reliable results, I needed to find an adequate size sample, which I knew would be a difficult challenge considering the relative scarcity and the lack of visibility of black/white interracial people. My initial efforts to find candidates for my project yielded no result. I had placed fliers at various college campuses describing the study. I put ads in three student newspapers and gave a brief talk at an African-American student organization—all in vain. After a period of considerable doubt as to whether this project was doable at all, I realized I had to be much more personal in my approach to finding participants. I elicited the help of several black and white professionals in nearby communities, as well as students and interracial families known to me. This produced a chain of referrals. Eventually I was invited to attend a newly formed organization for interracial students at a major university, where I met fifteen students who agreed to be interviewed. They in turn referred other organization members, fellow students, and interracial friends at various colleges and in other cities. Thus it was a word of mouth referral process or the "snowball" method that finally proved most effective in finding potential candidates for this project. Of the 122 participants that I eventually interviewed, three could not be included in the data. Two of these participants were below the age of eighteen, and the third looked interracial but had two socially defined black parents. The age range of the respondents was eighteen to thirty-five.

The 119 American-born black/white interracial young adults that I interviewed in the time span of one year came from all walks of life. The majority, however, were students. Many of them attended prestigious and private universities such as Harvard, Yale, Princeton, Columbia, Wesleyan, and Tufts. Some of the smaller private schools represented were Bucknell and Lock Haven universities and Marymount-Manhattan and Middlebury colleges. Although I made considerable effort to recruit participants from state and city colleges to obtain a more representative sample, these efforts were rewarded with only moderate success. A total of sixteen participants were obtained from state and city universities such as Rutgers, Hunter College, and City University of New York. The greater success in getting students from private universities may in part be attributed to the presence of formally recognized interracial student organizations. A few high school seniors participated in this study. Most of them attended public high schools. The rest of the study participants had a variety of backgrounds. There were housewives, teachers, administrators, delivery boys, orderlies, secretaries, executives, welfare mothers, city planners, computer experts, sales people, etc. Because many of the study respondents came from middle-class backgrounds, the sample was biased and not necessarily representative of the population at large.

All of the study respondents were the offspring of one black parent of African American roots and one white parent of European American descent. Ninety-three of the participants had black, two had interracial, and twenty-four had white fathers. None of the participants had interracial mothers but twenty-four had black and ninety-five had white mothers. The mean age was 21.4 years old. Most of the participants grew up in the northeastern part of the United States. However, several participants were from the Midwest and California. At the time of the interview all of them resided in northeastern states such as New York, New Jersey, Pennsylvania, Connecticut, Massachusetts, Washington, D.C., and Maryland. Most of the participants (89.1 percent) were single. (For details of demographic characteristics of the study respondents and their parents refer to Appendix A.)

The appearance of the men and women of this study showed a rainbow of colors. On one end of the color spectrum were medium-brown-skinned people and on the other end were fair-skinned people. More specifically, 11.8 percent of the study respondents had the overall appearance of a medium-brown black person, while 49.6 percent of them had the physical characteristics of a light-brown black person. Slightly more than a quarter (26.9 percent) of the respondents looked like dark-skinned white people and another 11.8 percent had the appearance of a fair-skinned white person.

Interviewing participants in the privacy of their homes generally worked the best, for there was little outside interference. The luxury of privacy, however, was frequently not available when interviewing students. Consequently, many interviews took place in dormitories, student lounges, empty classrooms, and libraries, cafes, diners, or restaurants. I compensated for occasional sound problems that interfered with getting good quality tape recordings by taking detailed notes.

Several methodological pathways were used to develop a portrait of the men and women who participated in this project. The *Brown Interracial Young Adult Interview* (Brown, 1991) was used as the principle instrument for this study. It examined racial identity, conflict, and the various experiential factors. The *Coopersmith Self-Esteem Inventory*, Adult Form (Coopersmith, 1987) measured their self-esteem. Finally, the *Spivey's Physical Characteristic Scale* (Spivey, 1984) focused on the appearance or phenotype of respondents. For the reader with an interest in a more detailed description of the instruments, reliability issues, and the interviewing process, I will discuss them briefly here.

The *Brown's Interracial Young Adult Interview*, which in absence of other interview schedules pertaining to interracial people, I constructed myself. This instrument is a semi-structured interview schedule consisting of sixty-seven questions and 256 variables. The content of this interview measured: (1) The degree to which the respondent identified as a black, white and/or interracial person; (2) The degree of conflict and uncertainty experienced in regard to racial identity; and (3) Certain experiences of the respondent within the family, community, and school and with peers/friends/dating partners and dating partners' parents. In particular, racial labeling, contact, acceptance, exposure to culture, and quality of relationships were examined. Questions with fixed alternative responses were posed to get factual information and data amenable to statistical analysis. Open-ended questions were used to obtain data pertaining to nuances of feelings, states, and experiences; to develop rapport between the researcher and participant and allow discussion of more "sensitive areas"; to clarify ambiguity and misunderstanding; and, finally, to note inconsistencies between verbal, written, and nonverbal responses. This approach enriched the study and provided in-depth information. The study consequently rendered qualitative as well as quantitative data. The interview schedule was completed by me on the basis of information obtained rather than giving that option to the respondent.

The interview worked quite well in regard to content validity and reliability. Many participants commented positively on the thoroughness and extent to which the instruments measured racial identity and their experiences as they related to the development of their racial identities. The interview seemed to stimulate memories, thoughts, and feelings in participants that they had forgotten or had failed to address previously. The cathartic effect of this experience appeared to be welcomed and appreciated.

Scale reliability for the *Brown Interracial Young Adult Interview*, as estimated by Cronbach's Alpha, was high for the racial identity scales (.84 to .76). The alphas of the experiential scales (contact, acceptance, and cultural exposure) ranged from high to adequate (.75 to .50). The exceptions were the "other people of color" scales and the black and white community acceptance scales, which had low inter-item reliability (below .50). However, because of the conceptual importance of the black and white community acceptance scales (.47 and .42 respectively) these scales were utilized in the study, while the "other people of color" scales (all below .45 and conceptually dispensable) were eliminated. The reasons for the low internal consistency of the "other people of color" scale may have been due to the concept being too broad and vague. Thus the operational definition may have included or excluded people in ways that were not intended. In turn, the low reliability scores in regard to black and white community acceptance may have been a reflection of participants' being more readily attuned to acceptance by select community members rather than the collective community. The concept may therefore also have been too broad and thus failed to measure more accurately what the researcher intended to measure.

The *Coopersmith Self-Esteem Inventory* (Adult Form) is a 25-item self-report questionnaire intended to measure the way a person evaluates and maintains an evaluation about him- or herself. The adult form is an adaptation of the school short form. Wording of the adult form was changed for eight items in order to reflect lifestyle and experiences for people over sixteen years of age. The adult form, which is scoreable for one scale, General-Self, contains both positive and negative statements about the self. Study participants responded to each of these items by indicating that the item is either "like me" or "unlike me."

According to Adair (1984) the Coopersmith self-esteem inventories are well researched, documented, and widely used. The school form, however, has been much more widely researched than either the short or the adult form. Kuder Richardson's internal consistency estimates (KR-20s) for the school form range from .87 to .92. Computed test-retest reliability estimates from college students who were administered the short form ranged from .80 for males to .82 for females. Studies of construct validity (Adair, 1984; Sewell, 1985) have shown the measure to correlate with reading achievement, perceived popularity, test anxiety, family adjustment, and the like. While no validity data are reported for the adult form, reliability estimates (Cronbach's alpha) ranged from .81 for different subsamples of college students (Coopersmith, 1987). This compares favorably with the Coopersmith Cronbach Alpha Reliabilities, which is .81 for the age range of twenty to thirty-four. The Cronbach alpha for this study was .80. Corrected item-total correlations ranged from .91 to .55.

Items from the *Spivey's Scale for Skin Color and Physical Characteristics* were used to assess the participant's skin color and physical characteristics. Spivey's measure has two parts. The first part of the measure provides a seven-item checklist measuring skin color, hair texture, eye color, and various facial features and body type. Each item was rated on a scale (varying from three to seven points). The second part of the measure gives a first impression of the participant's racial background on the basis of his or her total appearance, that is, the racial or ethnic background that would be assigned to the participant if his or her background were not known. The "First Impression" list has five items and was used for a more global impression of the participant's racial characteristics. The "First Impression" list yielded a more accurate measure of the participant's appearance than the itemized "Skin Color and Physical Characteristic Scale." Viewing certain physical characteristics in isolation could yield a distorted picture of the respondent. For instance, some had the coloring of a white person but the facial features, hair texture, body build, etc., of a black person. In contrast, a person could have the coloring of a light-brown black person but the facial features and hair type usually associated with a white person. These participants often looked more like a socially defined white person from the Mediterranean. I evaluated each participant for categorical inclusion immediately after the interview; therefore these ratings were subjective and did not profit from inter-rater reliability checks.

Before beginning the interviewing process, I would disclose that the topic to be discussed was of long-standing interest to me and originated from the experience of being in an interracial marriage and having raised two interracial children. I did this to diminish racial barriers and to facilitate the development of trust.

After the completion of the interview, I invited each respondent to elaborate on his or her feelings about the interview. I did this to make sure that the participant did not suffer any ill effects from having discussed personal and sometimes sensitive materials. This process was followed by my paying the participant the previously agreed hourly fee of $10.00. At times this fee was declined by the participant. A personal thank you note was then sent to each participant a few days after completion of the interview. The ethics of offering cash remuneration for interviews has always been controversial. However, I viewed it as showing respect for the interviewee's time and efforts and—especially for student participants with often little or no income—a welcomed gesture.

Jeanne Teresi and Douglas Holmes, who are highly regarded researchers with psychosocial issues of underserved populations, provided consultation and data analysis for the research project. Because of the general lack of knowledge about psychosocial issues of interracial children, a retrospective and cross-sectional design, rather than an experimental one, was chosen.

Limitation of Study

This study was intended to lay groundwork for more definitive studies. Rather than offering understanding into causal relationships, the data only give insight into certain phenomena and associations among various factors under investigation. Only a limited age group is being considered—the end of adolescence to young adulthood. Therefore generalization beyond that age group should not be made. Also, participants of this project reported their experiences from past events. Memories are unfortunately subject to distortions and may have biased the findings. Furthermore, the data generated from this project cannot be generalized to all interracial people. It is limited to United States–born interracial young adults. Further limitations relate to the characteristics of the sample that was biased in the direction of over sampling the more highly educated and middle class. A final limitation may have been the researcher's white racial and European cultural background. Study participants may have felt freer to expose their interracial or in some instances white identities than with a black researcher. However, they may have felt less comfortable in relating negative experiences with whites. Moreover, they may have refrained from talking about experiences that they felt embarrassed about, but may have discussed if the researcher had been interracial. While generalization of the results may be limited, I feel confident that this book will offer an in-depth look at the experience of growing up biracial in contemporary United States.

CHAPTER 3

Racism

In 1896, a judge explained, "The amalgamation of the races is not only unnatural, but is always productive of deplorable results. Our daily observation shows us, that the offsprings of these unnatural connections are generally sickly and effeminate, and that they are inferior in physical development and strength, to the full blood of either race" (Sickels, 1972, p. 48). Thus interracial couples and their children have been regarded as psychologically and socially abnormal. Racist attitudes against them have powerful psychological and sociological sources.

THE SIGNIFICANCE OF COLOR

Since the early history of man, color has played a major role in racial bigotry. The preference and the desire for light skin was, and continues to be, nearly universal. Roman Catholic rites held white to be the symbol of light, innocence, purity, and glory. Sacred horses in Greek, Roman, Celtic, and Germanic cultures were usually white (Cirlot, 1971). White represented the duality of day and night. In the progression of darkness to lightness, the rising of the sun dissolves darkness and mystery of the night. Whiteness in this duality symbolizes masculinity or a superior force.

In contrast, black is associated with the ocean, the unconscious, the mysterious, and the feminine. Cirlot (1971) included in the forces of blackness the states of "fermentation, putrefaction, occultation and penitence," which are regarded in mysticism as negative and dark forces. Traditionally, people have been classified into four distinct color categories. The four major categories are red, white, yellow, and black. Pigmentation has also been used to classify people into caste, religious, and social groups.

Throughout the United States, Central and South America, Asia, and even Africa, there has been prejudice against those with darker skin. In a race-stratified society like that of America, the implications of such prejudice are enormous. Before the Civil War the difference between light and dark skin could mean the difference between being a free or an enslaved person. Pigmentation and racial features continue to influence who will be rich, poor, educated, beautiful, or plain (Russell, Wilson and Hall, 1992).

Dark-skinned black men frequently have been able to counteract discrimination based on color with special talents, intelligence, and education. This has been much less possible for women who live in a world where the beauty of a woman counts as much as physical prowess, intelligence, or financial security matters in men. With the American beauty ideal being fair skin, blond hair, and blue or green eyes, dark-skinned black women have been especially vulnerable to color prejudice. Consequently, throughout history, black women have looked for formulas and techniques to lighten their skin, straighten their hair, and make their features "less Negroid" looking. Black literature frequently focuses on the pain experienced by black women regarding darkness. In Wallace Thurman's 1929 book, *The Blacker the Berry*, the dark-skinned Emma Lou poignantly describes her feeling about her skin color:

She should have been a boy, then color of skin wouldn't have mattered so much, for wasn't her mother always saying that a black boy could get along, but that a black girl would never know anything but sorrow and disappointment? But she wasn't a boy; she was a girl, and color did matter, mattered so much that she would rather have missed receiving her high school diploma than have to sit as she now sat, the only odd and conspicuous figure on the auditorium platform of the Boise high school. (p. 21)

For centuries black women have equated dark skin with rejection and suffering and light skin with acceptance and love. The envy, jealousy, and competition between dark- and light-skinned women can be enormous. In Toni Morrison's *The Bluest Eye*, the dark-skinned Claudia receives an Aryan-looking doll for Christmas. She responds with rage.

I destroy white baby dolls. . . . But the dismembering of dolls was not the true horror. The true horrifying thing was the transference of the same impulses to little white girls. The indifference with which I could have axed them was shaken only by my desire to do so. To discover what eluded me: the secret of the magic they weaved on others. What made people look at them and say, "Awwwww," but not for me? (p. 22)

Black psychiatrists (Grier and Cobbs, 1968) have noted that every American black girl experiences some degree of shame about the way she looks. Their self-worth becomes linked to the lightness of their skin, caucasian-like features, and to whether they have "good" or "kinky" hair. From early childhood on, they must undergo painful hair-combing ordeals that are geared toward making them look more like the white beauty ideal. Thus the importance of skin color has not only been derived from biology, but skin tones have played an important role in classifying and organizing the social, cultural, and psychological worlds. The impact of this organization had devastating consequences for both blacks and interracial people.

IMPACT OF RACISM ON BLACKS

Ralph Ellison, in his 1952 book *The Invisible Man*, powerfully captures the outrage, pain, and frustrations experienced by black people, the victims of racist thinking. Ellison writes:

I am an invisible man. No, I am not a spook like those who haunted Edgar Allen Poe; nor am I one of your Hollywood movie echo plasma. I am a man of substance, of flesh and bone, fiber and liquids and I might even be said to possess a mind. I am invisible, understand, simply because people refuse to see me. When they approach me they see only my surroundings, themselves, figments of their imagination—indeed, everything and anything except me. (p. 19)

James Baldwin, in a talk to New York City teachers in 1963, said:

It is not really a "Negro Revolution" that is upsetting this country. What is upsetting the country is a sense of its own identity. Where we are now is that a whole country of people believe I am a "nigger" and I don't and the battle is on. Because if I am not what I have been told I am, then it means that you're not what you thought you were either. And that is the crisis.

Studies that examined the impact of racism on the personality of blacks before the emergence of the Black Power movement paint a bleak picture. These early scholars also noted the predominance among minorities of identification with the dominant race, as well as the preference to be white.

Abram Kardiner and Lionel Ovesey (1951) suggest that a basic personality for blacks really does exist because of the specific social conditions to which they must adapt. The black personality, according to these authors, is a caricature of the white personality in the sense that the social goals of blacks and whites are similar, but blacks are deprived of the means to reach them. Constantly receiving unfavorable images of themselves takes a tremendous psychological toll, especially of their self-esteem. Kardiner and Ovesey write that blacks encounter much conflict over the question, Who do I want to be like? The parental ideal is blemished because of the social devaluation they have suffered. Blacks cannot embrace a white ideal because they can never become white, although attempts are made, with the aid of cosmetics and hair straighteners, to approximate this ideal. The more they accept this white ideal, however, the greater the psychic conflict. Consequently, the psychological quest for an ideal is doomed to failure. Kardiner and Ovesey suggest that the conflict is especially intense for middle-class blacks who push themselves in terms of accomplishments and thus are closer to reaching the white ideal.

Helen McLean (1963) concurs with this view of the traumatic effects of racism on blacks. She also points to the important conditioning that blacks undergo from childhood to be subservient toward white people. If humiliated by whites, they must cover up their rage. Analysis of blacks, according to McLean, reveals much self-loathing and the wish to be white. Consequently, racism has a powerful impact on black identity formation. In his 1963 book *Childhood and Society*, Eric Erikson observes that black people are subjected not only to the bodily tensions, conflicts, and anxiety inherent in everybody's developmental process but also to the distress caused by what is done to them by the dominant group. Their ego and even their bodies may consequently be subjected to an excessive amount of tension, pain, and anxiety. Prevented from participation in the collective strength of mainstream America, they may either overtly or covertly take on the role of outsider or struggle for a place among the dominant group. The social pressures encountered in this process might have an impact on both their physical and their emotional health. Erikson writes that the social environment allows black people to live only at the expense of a permanent loss of identity. He points to the inevitable identification with the dominant race and the attempt of the "master race to protect their own identity against the very sensual and oral temptations emanating from the race held to be inferior." In this restrictive social milieu, three identities are formed, according to Erikson:

(1) Mammy's oral—sensual "honey child"—tender, expressive, rhythmical; (2) the evil identity of the dirty, anal-sadistic, phallic-rapist "nigger"; and (3) the clean, anal-compulsive, restrained, friendly but always sad "white man's Negro." (p. 242)

Erikson suggests that migration to the North did not improve the predicament of blacks; it only imposed more subtle restrictions. In essence, it threatened the identity of slaves, which was their only historically successful identity. The so-called greater opportunities of the North, according to Erikson, did not accomplish a reintegration of the identity fragments mentioned earlier.

Kenneth and Mamie Clark were the first black researchers who systematically examined racial awareness and identity issues in black children. In their famous 1947 study, they looked at the effects of race preference on the self-concept of black children. The researchers gave the children in their sample a choice between four dolls, two black and two white, with distinct racial features. The subjects of this experiment were 253 black children, 134 from segregated public nursery schools, and 119 from racially mixed nursery schools. The Clarks found that black children preferred white dolls and rejected black dolls when asked to choose which were nice, which were bad, which they would like to play with, and which was a nice color. The Clarks concluded from their findings that black children would rather be white.

Studies that emerged during the Civil Rights movement confirmed the Clark's findings. The Greenwald and Oppenheimer study (1968) replicated the racial doll study with white as well as black children who were given a choice of three rather than two dolls with different skin colors. Both black and white children rejected the colored dolls when asked such questions as "Is there a doll that is a good doll?" The majority of the children preferred the white doll to play with, thought it was the good doll, and believed it to have a nice color. Greenwald and Oppenheimer conclude that black children do not manifest an unusual tendency to misidentify themselves but that the black skin color is undesirable to them.

Many of the studies conducted in the 1970s, when the effects of black consciousness raising became widespread, failed to verify earlier findings. Joseph Hraba and Geoffrey Grant (1970) demonstrated that both black and white children showed a consistency in their preference for their own race and that black children who are part of interracial settings do not necessarily demonstrate a white orientation. The authors suggest that this change in attitudes might be the result of blacks' increasing pride in their race due to black pride campaigns. Another possible explanation is that cross-racial contact may foster pride in being black. S. H. Ward and J. Braun's findings (1972) continued to produce results that were quite different from those of the Clark studies. Studying the relationship between self-esteem and racial preference in black children, they found that the majority of black children preferred the black puppet. Seventy percent saw it as the "nice puppet," 28 percent saw the black puppet as having a nice color, and 79 percent said the white puppet "looked bad." The middle-class black children did not show a greater preference for the white puppet than did the lower-class children. Like Hraba and Grant, Ward and Braun attribute these changing results to an uplift in racial pride and identity fostered by the social and political movements that many blacks were deeply involved with. As the authors explain, "Possibly such changes or movements might contribute to increased feelings of competence, and encourage blacks to identify with or adopt their own group as a social comparison model" (p. 664).

In 1971, William Cross responded to the call for developing a black psychology that would take into consideration the experiences of people within the context of black Americans, in particular their psychosocial, economic, and cultural environments. Cross, theorizing from a black psychological perspective, developed a five-stage developmental model through which black people progress on their path toward a racial identity. He called this model the "Negro to Black/Conversion Experience." Cross calls these stages pre-encounter (pre-discovery) stage, encounter (discovery) stage, immersion-emersion stage, internalization stage, and finally, the commitment stage. In the pre-encounter stage the person has anti-black attitudes, devalues blacks, and has a white Euro-American frame of reference that dominates his behavior and his thinking and feeling patterns. During the encounter stage the old belief system is challenged by an occurrence in the social or political realm that makes the person receptive to reevaluating his beliefs about blacks as well as his own identity. In the immersion-emersion stage, the person embraces the world of blackness. There is a celebration of the deep involvement in black culture, idealization of blacks and a devaluing and dehumanizing of whites. The person may join the Muslims or join in rap sessions during this phase. There may be concern over whether he is "black enough." In the fourth stage, internalization, the person not only begins to live according to a new self-image, but "becomes a new identity" (p. 23). Confidence builds in his personal values as a black person, and the uncontrolled rage toward whites changes to controlled and conscious anger towards racist and oppressive practices. The final stage of Cross's developmental model is the commitment stage which is characterized by the person's active commitment to social change that will enhance and improve the lives of black people.

Two studies conducted by D. Powell-Hopson (1985) and S. Gopaul-McNicol (1986) suggest a reversal of emotional benefits that was associated with the "Black Is Beautiful" movement. The outcome of their study parallels the findings of the Clarks several decades earlier. It is unclear whether this similarity is due to the more conservative social climate of the 1980s or to the two researchers' reliance on a close adaptation of the Clarks's doll choice instrument. The findings of the two Hopson and Gopaul-McNicol studies, one conducted in the United States, the other in Trinidad, again showed that black preschool children preferred the white skin colors. The children tested were shown black and white Cabbage Patch dolls and asked which they preferred. In the United States, two thirds of the 155 black children that Powell-Hopson studied preferred the white dolls, while in Trinidad 85 percent of the light-skinned black children and 64 percent of dark-skinned black children preferred the white doll. In response to these findings, St. Elmo Gopaul, Secretary General of the Trinidad and Tobago teacher's union, said at a news conference that despite Trinidadians being 85 percent black and having a black government, Trinidad has not recovered from the four hundred years in which blacks knew that whites were in charge. The two researchers conclude that feelings of racial inferiority continue to be as intense as they were forty years ago.

Steinhorn and Diggs (2000) view integration in the United States as a myth. While they acknowledge the progress made by blacks in the last fifty years, they challenge the belief of many whites that discrimination is a thing of the past. In a rather wrenching conclusion they write, "Integration is an illusion born of hope and desire, that our devotion to the ideal ironically helps us to avoid a real reckoning on race, and that for our nation to move beyond today's racial endgame we must relinquish the hope of ever reaching the Promised Land" (p. 250). To achieve a color-blind nation these authors urge that America must give up its illusion that real integration has taken place.

In summary, the literature has repeatedly shown that black children exhibit preference for the white dominant group membership. While the Black Power movement seemed to have brought an amelioration and reversal to these problems, the more conservative social climate that began to emerge in the nineties suggests that the problems of racism and its impact on racial identity development and self-esteem are reemerging. The brutal murder of a black man in Jasper, Texas, in June 1998, was not seen as an aberration by John Hope Franklin, a distinguished historian. Franklin observed that such tragedies occur periodically. In July 1998, Bill Cosby's wife wrote after the murder of her son that racism is "omnipresent and eternalized in America's institutions, media and myriad entities."

While positive changes in America's race relations have been made during the last fifty years, Camille Cosby's indictment echoes the feeling of many African Americans that serious racial division is by no means a past event.

RACISM AGAINST INTERRACIAL PEOPLE

In 1994, a high school principal in Alabama was in the national limelight after he threatened to cancel the prom if students brought dates from a different race. When an interracial student asked the principal whom he could bring to the prom, the principal replied, "That's the problem. Your mom and dad shouldn't have had you. You were a mistake" (Smothers, 1994).

The abhorrence against racial mixing that many whites have harbored in this country is perhaps best captured in the name they invented for interracial people. The term "mulatto" according to the Random House Dictionary of the English Language is:

1. The sterile offspring of a female horse and a male donkey, valued as a work animal, having strong muscles, a body shaped like a horse, and donkey like large ears, small feet, and surefootedness. 2. Any hybrid between the donkey and the horse. 3. *Informal.* A very stubborn person. 4. Bot. any sterile hybrid.

Judy Scales-Trent, in her recent book *Notes of a White Black Woman* (1995), responds with outrage at the degradation implied by this term. She writes:

"Sterile hybrid"—What a ghastly term to apply to a person. It describes the result of a sexual union so unnatural, by species so unlike, that this creature is unable to meet one of the basic criteria of a species—the ability to reproduce. It describes a creature that will, happily, *not* be able to continue its unnatural line—a being that will die without offspring, so that the category "horse" and "donkey" ("white," "black") will return to their former state of purity.

Sexual license across boundaries, with no social consequences—this is the dream of America. (p. 100)

James Baldwin poignantly addresses the racist distortion implied in the term "mulatto." In his book *The Evidence of Things Not Seen* (1985) he comments, "It is impossible to look on a man and pretend that this man is a mule. It is impossible to couple with a Black woman and describe the child you have both created as a mulatto—either it's your child, or a child, or it isn't" (p. 31).

Scientific and social theories regarding interracial people have been based for the most part on impressionistic rather than empirical evidence. During slavery, being half white made interracial people, in the eyes of social scientists and the public, superior to their uniracial black counterparts. Their physical attractiveness was frequently praised, and they were considered more intelligent than blacks. After abolition, however, the image of the mulatto was changed drastically. Biological and sociocultural arguments consistently portrayed them as degenerates and as dangerous (Berzon, 1978). Both theories severely damaged the image of interracial people in this country (Nakashima, 1992).

At the center of the biological argument is the "hybrid degeneracy" theory, which started around the end of the Civil War and was prevalent until the mid-1930s. Interracial people, according to the hybrid degeneracy theory, were supposedly emotionally unstable and biologically inferior to both their racially homogeneous black and white parents. This theory was widely popular among the public as well as scholars. For example, the French psychologist Gustave le Bon wrote in 1912, "Mixed breeds are ungovernable" (quoted in Barzun, 1937/1965, p. 227). The American sociologist Edward Reuter (1931/1969) contended that "the mixed blood" is [by definition] an unadjusted person (p. 216). Provine (1973), quoting Charles Benedict Davenport, the one-time "leading" advocate of eugenics in the United States, wrote, "One often sees in mulattos an ambition and push combined with intellectual inadequacy which makes the unhappy hybrid dissatisfied with his lot and a nuisance to others" (p. 366).

Their "unnatural blend" (Krauss, 1941) supposedly made mulattos depressed, moody, irrational, discontent, impulsive, confused, nervous, etc. (Berzon, 1978; Bogle, 1989; Elfenbein, 1989; Scheick, 1979; Stedman, 1982). Within this belief system, racially mixed people supposedly would suffer an early death because of their physical, mental, emotional, and moral weakness. Mulattos were also believed to be "criminal, sterile, not harmoniously proportioned in body, more prone to tuberculosis and to childbirthing difficulties" than whites or blacks (Myrdal, 1944, p. 197).

Their physical characteristics were described as bordering at times on the grotesque. According to Provine (1973), scientists hypothesized that the circulatory systems of interracial people are too long or too big for their body size (Provine, 1973). Their bodies, arms, and legs are not in harmonious proportion, and their teeth are too big or too small for their mouth. Fleming (1939) who conducted a highly questionable scientific study of mixed-race children in England reported that 10 percent of the black/white mixed children had a well-arched jaw from the Negro side and a badly arch jaw from the white side" (p. 68).

The literary critic Sterling Brown (1933) explained that the stereotypes held by whites regarding mulattos were based on several racist premises.

First, the mulatto inherits the vices of both races and none of the virtues; second, any achievement of a Negro is to be attributed to the White blood in his vein. The logic runs that even inheriting the worst from whites is sufficient for achievement in Negroes. The mulatto is a victim of a divided inheritance; from his White blood come his intellectual strivings, his unwillingness to be a slave; from his Negro blood come his baser emotional urges, his indolence, his savagery. (p. 194)

The religious component of this theory—that what is "unnatural" is not condoned by God—strengthened and popularized the argument of genetic inferiority.

The sociocultural argument described mixed-race people as marginal. Supposedly, they were tormented and confused by the two conflicting cultures they harbored within themselves. Park (1928) coined the phrase "marginal man" for a person trapped between two worlds but belonging in neither. Stonequist (1937), a student of Park, described the mulatto as a "racial hybrid" caught in the search for identity and struggling for survival between contemporary destructive forces. For Fleming (1930), Park (1931) and W. C. Smith (1939), mulattos were social outcasts because they were not fully accepted by either blacks or whites. Fiction, theater, film, and the scholarly community seemed to agree with the depiction of the "tragic mulatto." From Thomas Nelson Page to D. W.

Griffith to William Faulkner, children of interracial couples were invariably described as lost souls (Spickard, 1989, p. 329). Abolitionists used the image of the "tragic mulatto" as a deterrent to the institution of slavery (Berzon, 1978; Dearborn, 1986; Elfenbein, 1989).

The Black Power movement with its celebration of cultural and ethnic differences brought about a turning point in the interracial mythology. There was an increasing recognition that all people of color and some whites in the United States are biracial to various degrees and that this could be an enriching rather than a marginalizing experience (Blauner, 1972; Steinberg, 1981). Social scientists began to talk about the "issues" of interracial people rather than their "problems" (Chang, 1974; Diene and Vinacke, 1964; Gibbs, 1987; Johnson and Nagoshi, 1986). Interracial people were now described as "children of the future" capable of bridging the gap that has been created by whites because of its racist abuses against people of color. They were seen as socially adept, moving with ease in both the black and white world and having a keen worldview (Adams, 1973; Nakashima, 1992; Poussaint, 1984).

The Black Power movement also benefited mixed-race people in that it taught pride in blackness. Finally, it brought about the recognition that racial group cohesion is an important means to obtaining political, social, and economic power and that assimilation is oppressive to people of color. However, the movement also had serious drawbacks for mixed-race people. For the rejection of the assimilation of blacks into white culture was paralleled with the rejection of interracial marriage and its children. People of color who married cross-racially were considered "traitors" or "sellouts."

Among these voices were a few who pointed out the underlying racist premise of the "one drop of black blood" rule. For instance, Alvin Poussaint (1984) wrote:

Blackness . . . is very strong stuff. One drop makes you Black. Blackness is impurity and whiteness is purity, and any impurity introduced into purity makes the whole thing impure. In that way, whites preserve white supremacy and relegate the tainted ones to the lower caste. It's very confusing to us Americans, although we accept the definition, and it's also very confusing to biracial children. (p. 10)

Racial categories have become a social and political tool that separates and excludes rather than a means of describing the traits of a group by its anatomical and psychological characteristics or its phenotypes. The pressure to pigeonhole oneself into a box too small to reflect a multiracial makeup has disappeared. However, the tradition to define people by blood quantum is so much a part of the American way of life that the effort to assure the civil rights of interracial people will have to go far beyond a change in officially recognized racial categories.

THE NATURE OF RACISM

Social scientists have long understood that race is not a biological problem but is created by psychological and social forces alone. Martin Bergman, a distinguished psychoanalyst who studied anti-Semitic attitudes, concluded that anti-Semitism was unrelated to a specific character pathology but rather was related to stranger anxiety or something similar deeply embedded in the human psyche. Francis Montague and Ashley Montague (1940) explained that race prejudice allows individuals to free themselves of internal tensions. For instance, aggressive or hostile feelings are projected or displaced onto some group or a person viewed as representing that group. Anger, frustrations, humiliation and subsequent feelings of aggression suffered during childhood, adolescence or adulthood usually underlie racial bigotry. If society permits the attachment of these feelings to a group of people, racist attitudes will be facilitated and will provide a welcome release for uncomfortable or intolerable internal tensions. Moskovitz (1998) also regards racism as projections: He writes:

The potential for racism is deep and universal, but is nurtured by context and leadership. . . . I have come to see racism from a more Kleinian perspective. The depressive position, a position that entails owning one's hatred, is always a struggle to maintain. It is always easier to see badness in others than in ourselves. (p. 363)

Traits that cause guilt or shame such as sexual impulses, aggression, and hostility are especially prone to be split off and projected or displaced onto others, from one person to another—that is, onto a group identified by race (Money-Kyrle, 1960). Like other minority groups, interracial people are prime targets for these split-off parts. They have been labeled by dominant groups as immoral, uncivilized, sexually out of control, criminal, etc.

Another important force that frequently underlies racist attitudes is the resistance to recognizing differences that might result in feelings of confusion and distress. Thus, we ignore evidence that might change our belief system, since new evidence may upset our psychic equilibrium.

An important remedy to racism is helping people become integrated human beings.

Race has been used to justify slavery, colonization, segregation, and genocide. The Nazis justified the policy of mass extermination of the Jewish people through the manipulation of scientific facts. Generally, racial purity laws are attributed to the racist doctrines of Nazi Germany and South Africa. America, however, also had racial purity laws. They existed from the early colonies through the early 1980s (see chapter 2). Two major reversals occurred on the issue of race in both the European and American scientific community. The first took place in the 1930s, when scientists made passionate pleas against race crossing, claiming that it produced physically and mentally inferior people. The second change came during and after World War II, when the world recognized how scientific research was exploited in Nazi Germany in an attempt to demonstrate the detrimental effects of race mixing. The horrible toll that resulted from Nazi racist doctrines contributed to the reversal of scientific writings.

Pettigrew (1964) insisted that pure races in man had never existed and, further, cannot exist, since racial mixing has taken place since ancient times. According to Pettigrew, racist theories are based on "biological Gresham's law—the bad drives out the good" (p. 62). Pettigrew (1964) also challenged the belief that harmful biological effects are the result of cross mating. Swiss villagers, for example, found that intermarriage with neighboring villagers resulted in taller offspring.

New scientific understanding about race seems to have had little effect in bringing about a reconsideration of the way we think about race. For example, scientists are increasingly challenging the notion of race as type. Alice Brues (1977) wrote that race is a "division of a species which differs from other divisions by the frequency with which certain hereditary traits appear among its members" (p. 1). This definition defies the notion of racial makeup as being exclusionary or having clear boundaries. Cooper and David (1986) pointed out that the biological concept of race was intended to clarify and describe human differences. However, the uncritical acceptance of this concept and the absence of consistent definitions based on phenotypes represent a problem even in the field of biology.

Research based on reliable genetic evidence is for various reasons largely missing (Provine, 1973). The revulsion that many educated Americans and people all over the world felt in response to Nazi race doctrines was one of the primary reasons scientists refrained from conducting research that would have produced reliable genetic evidence on the subject of human race mixing. Another reason for the reluctance of scientists to conduct research in this area is that controlled race mixing is difficult to arrange. Finally, scientists seem to hesitate to conduct experiments that would take three human generations to complete in order to produce scientifically valid data.

Despite some of the new insights gained in regard to race mixing, we have continued to define racial group membership according to racial purity laws. When Hawaii became the fiftieth state, the U.S. Census Bureau imposed its categories on a population that up to then had recorded populations according to categories and mixtures that reflected its multiracial population. As Nakashima (1992) pointed out, "U.S. society operates under a monoracial hegemonic culture in which race is seen as something solid and immutable" (p. 175). In light of the "browning of America," these traditions are becoming increasingly outdated. Moreover, interracial people have been forced to live with the inadequacies and the complications of this system. The increasing voices that have challenged the racist premise that underlies this country's concept of racial group belonging are finally being heard.

CHAPTER 4

Racial Identity, Conflict, and Self-esteem

RACIAL IDENTITY

Obviously, racial self-perception is not something that is inborn or hard-wired like computer technology. Rather, it is formed through the ongoing interaction with a person's immediate and extended social environment (Erikson, 1963). The awareness of one's racial group is established by the age of four or five (Piskacek and Golub, 1973; Tatum, 1997 and Warner, 1987). Because children know at that stage that their color will not change, they experience ambivalence and their exploration of the meaning of identity begins. The process of exploration will be positive if the parents foster healthy ego development. As interracial children grow up, the parents should encourage them to embrace both parts of their racial heritage, accept evidence of identity fluctuations, and raise them in a racially mixed community.

Once the children immerse themselves in the wider social milieu, they begin to identify with groups of people whose physical characteristics, attitudes, racial values, and mores are different from their own and those of their immediate surroundings. Family and societal communications about who the child is racially become increasingly intertwined and influence the child's perceptions about his or her place within a multitude of different racial groups. Thus, racial identity development becomes a dynamic process facilitated by the interaction between the child, parent, and society at large.

Within each of these systems the interracial child is confronted with various emotional challenges that are different for them than for uniracial black or white children. First, the child has to understand the concept "interracial." This label is more abstract than "Black," "White," or "Asian" categories and is therefore more difficult to assimilate (Jacobs, 1977). The understanding of this label is further complicated when both parents are from racially homogenous backgrounds. Simultaneously, with the assimilation of the "Interracial" label, racially mixed children are expected to integrate the knowledge that society regards them as black.

Assuming a black racial identity poses yet another set of emotional hurdles that are difficult to surmount, even for black children of uniracial parents. Black children must incorporate the prevalent values of our society, which include the devaluation of black people. They also must incorporate the mores and culture of the black community, and these frequently clash with the values of white society (McAdoo, 1985). Interracial children may experience this clash of cultures particularly intensely, since they harbor both black and white racial heritages within themselves. For them, assuming a black identity means negating the socially idealized white in favor of the socially disparaged black part. Becoming black may be associated with fears of being abused, terrorized, and discriminated against. Consequently, resistance to embracing the black identity may not only be related to unwillingness to disassociate themselves from their whiteness but to apprehension about what it means to be black in a country that has historically oppressed black people.

The lack of interracial families and specific cultural practices or values with which to identify leaves interracial children without a reference group. Therefore, an interracial group identification often becomes intangible (Spickard, 1992) and leaves them with a sense of being alone, isolated, or marginal. Conflict may also arise from feelings of being different from their white or black parent or other uniracial siblings or playmates. If the phenotype of these children is neither clearly white or black, they may be subjected to curious stares and constant questions about their racial group. Such curiosities emphasize the perception of being marginal.

Finally, the historical antagonism between blacks and whites can prevent the integration of identity fragments that represent the oppressor and the oppressed. A twenty-two-year-old religion major explained, "It's difficult to have ancestors who are slaves and slave owners. It's a strange paradox. Something isn't right here. It doesn't go together. But it's all part of my heritage. How to make sense of that is very difficult." Thus racial identity formation requires the negotiation of various emotional hazards.

Because the path toward a racial identity for biracial children is complex, it does not necessarily follow a linear progression toward blackness as has been commonly assumed (Adams, 1973; Drake and Cayton, 1945). Rather, racial identity formation in black/white mixed children seems to be a multidimensional process influenced by experiential, physical, personal, and demographic factors in addition to personal inclinations. The process itself consists of identity variation, public versus private identities, primary and secondary identities, and identity fluctuations (Brown, 1991, 1995, and 1997).

Identity Variations

Racial identity varies among mixed-race people. As the findings of this study showed, some study participants saw themselves as black, a few as white, but the majority had interracial identities (for details, see Table 2). The prevalence of the interracial identity among respondents was not surprising. For biracial children are not just black or just white; rather they incorporate both black and white identity parts in one body and one self. Similarly, given the consistent societal conditioning toward blackness and the message that the white identity is a taboo, the frequency of these identities also were of little surprise. The expectation to disregard half of themselves was an almost impossible challenge for many participants. As one young student explained, "When you mix salt and pepper, it's impossible to separate the grains. You have a new spice, not just salt and not just pepper. The same is true when you are interracial." The few participants who chose the "Other" category on forms frequently added that they were interracial, biracial, mulatto, or human beings.

Public versus Private Identities

The most common adaptation to the socially imposed identity restrictions was a compartmentalization of a public and private identity. Rather

Table 2

Public versus Private Racial Identities

(n = 119)

CATEGORY CHOICE	Public (%)	Private (%)
Black	64.7	19.3
White	0.8	5.0
Hispanic	0.8	---
Asian	---	---
Native American	---	---
Other	33.6	5.9
Interracial	---	66.4
Undecided	---	3.4

*Columns add to 100% (except where due to rounding error.)

than denying their whiteness, participants frequently were in "the closet" with their interracial or, in some instances, forbidden white identities. Publicly, they defined themselves as black. Thus almost two thirds (64.7 percent) of the respondents chose the black racial category on forms requesting racial group membership information. However, in the absence of external pressures, slightly more than two thirds (66.4 percent) indicated that they would identify themselves as interracial, while a few (5 percent) said they would define themselves as white. The compartmentalization of a public and private identity helped many participants to balance societal expectations with their own racial self-perceptions. Feeling pressured to misidentify themselves and hide their true identities, as are gays, was an ongoing emotional irritant for many of the men and women. Moreover, it pressured them toward identity restriction rather than a synthesis of black and white identity parts.

For some, the conversion from a public to a private identity seemed to be the result of a gradual conditioning process in which they consistently received the message that they were black rather than interracial or white. For others, it was a conscious and sudden decision after a traumatic experience in which their identities came under fire. Jo Ann, a twenty-three-year-old college senior, whose strong interracial identity was challenged in college when she began taking a Black Awareness course, explained:

I did not have a problem until someone said: "Well, how can you consider yourself interracial? You are black!" That was in my Black Awareness class. (The professor was trying to get us to say whether we consider ourselves as black or white.) "You can't be both" [the professor explained]. So I said, "Well, I am both, you can't tell me I am not!" So he said: "If there was a war, blacks are on one side and whites are on the other side, which side would you go on?" I said: "Probably neither, because I would have to choose between my father and mother and I don't have a favorite." But since I could not answer, he was yelling at me, "People see you as black." "That is just describing my color," Jo Ann responded, "but if I go by what I know, I can't consider myself black." I remember I was very upset and I wanted to drop out of class after that. But ever since then I have been filling out forms by what people see me as [black] rather than what I should put down. I decided I did not want to have any more confrontations. I know a lot of my friends are the same way. Well, my black friends anyway. I don't want to have every single day an argument.

Thus to avoid social hardships by coming out of the closet, many interracial people exercise control over the disclosure. This control seems to be adaptive. Crohn (1995), who interviewed some black/white mixed-race students in a group setting, found a similar phenomenon. Eight out of the ten students identified themselves exclusively as black in the group setting, but in one-to-one interviews, results changed to the opposite. Eight out of ten said they identified mostly as interracial.

Pressures to adopt black identities were not always restricted to external forces. Failure to negate their whiteness seemed to elicit guilt and shame for betraying black parents, relatives, and friends. Some felt disloyal to blacks in general or to the principles of the Black Power movement. Denying their white roots seemed no less painful. As Jo Ann's account demonstrates, it was frequently equated with hiding their white parent or other white relatives. In addition, it represented the negation of social, economic, and psychological advantages associated with the white world.

Primary and Secondary Identities

Many participants identified to different degrees with all three identity options, to the parts as well as the sum of their racial heritages (refer to Table 3). Consequently, there were primary and secondary identities.

Table 3

Primary and Secondary Racial Identities

(n = 119)

Degree of Identifications	BLACK (%)	WHITE (%)	INTERRACIAL (%)
Not at all	3.4	20.1	2.5
Somewhat	48.7	63.9	26.1
Very much	47.9	16.0	71.4

Columns add to 100% (except where due to rounding error).

This is not surprising since the racial makeup of participants was different from that of their racially homogeneous black and white parents, a difference that frequently seemed to make complete racial identification with either parent difficult. The black identity and particularly the white identity (an illegal identity for interracial people, even if they look white) often, though not always, emerged as secondary. In contrast, the interracial identity, reflecting the actual dual racial makeup of participants, often emerged as primary. It seems that the reality of their mixed racial background often overshadowed societal pressures toward blackness or the lure toward whiteness. Thus many participants were able to hold on to an identity nucleus that most closely represented their genetic and psychic being. Nevertheless, the constant pressures toward over-identification with the minority parent posed an ongoing threat to a natural course of identity development.

Identity Fluctuations

Identity has been defined as "the relatively enduring, but not necessarily stable, experience of the self as a unique, coherent entity over time" (Moore and Fine, 1991). Because interracial children must negotiate a multitude of emotional hazards in their quest of a racial identity and are subjected to constant pressures to misidentify themselves, their racial self-perceptions seem less stable than those of uniracial children.

As Table 4 illustrates, racial identity in the men and women of this study fluctuated during the various developmental phases. The black,

Table 4

Racial Identity During Various Developmental Periods

(n = 119)

Race	Black	White	Interracial	Other	Not Sure
Time					
Pre-School	16.8%	14.3%	19.3%	2.5%	47.1%
Grade School	25.2	21.8	33.6	3.4	16.0
High School	29.4	10.9	54.6	----	5.0
After High School	29.4	4.2	57.1	----	9.2

Rows add to 100% (except where due to a rounding error.)

and particularly the interracial identity, seemed to grow progressively stronger from the preschool to the post-high-school years. According to this albeit retrospective data, many of the interviewees viewed themselves as interracial rather than black as they grew older. In contrast, the white identity seemed to weaken through the course of development. Apparently, the claim to their white parent's racial heritage was increasingly abandoned as the American color hierarchy became absorbed.

The degree of identity fluctuations seemed to be strongly influenced by social factors. A nineteen-year-old student who lived with his white mother after his parents were divorced explained, "When I was growing up, I did not have a problem with race. I was a black interracial child in a mostly white neighborhood. When I moved to New Jersey at age twelve, I was thrown into a mostly all-black neighborhood and black school. It was a shock. I really had to look at myself. I was no longer sure who I was racially. I was very much white on the inside and very different than the black kids in the neighborhood. I learned to fight and got my butt beat a lot. I began to act, speak, walk, and think black. I adopted their attitudes, saw myself as part of the black group, different from whites. This changed again when I moved to E. and went to a white school."

Iris, who looked like a dark-skinned white woman, recalled, "It comes in cycles. It changes all the time. Until I was four years old, I wanted to be black and have nappy hair like everybody else. We were living in a black neighborhood. So my mother bought me a wig one year. That made me very happy. Then there was a period in junior high school and

Table 5

Conflict and/or Uncertainty about Racial Identity

(n = 119)

MEASURE	CONFLICT (%)
None	23.5
Large Extent	31.9
Somewhat	42.9
Not Sure	1.7

Column adds to 100% (except where due to a rounding error.)

I remember wanting to be white, because most of the people there were white. I would be uncomfortable when my black stepfather would show up. Now I have problems not being accepted as a black woman. So it is a real difficult thing."

CONFLICT

The potential for conflict was present in all three racial identities. The interracial identity has just begun to be officially sanctioned in the United States, and the black or white identity only reflects half of the biracial person's heredity. In addition, the white identity defies racial purity laws. It was, therefore, not surprising that the majority of participants (74.8 percent) had experienced conflict and/or uncertainty about their racial identity while growing up (see Table 5).

The degree of conflict associated with each of the three identity options differed. The white identity was the most costly in emotional terms (see Table 6). However, the common assumption that the black identity is the most successful racial identity for interracial people could not be confirmed. The black identity tended to correlate only with insignificant conflict reduction.

In contrast, the interracial identity was associated with significantly diminished conflict. Since the interracial identity most closely reflected the actual racial makeup of the study participants and did not require the denial of their true racial selves, the interracial identity seemed to be the one most conducive to their emotional well-being.

Table 6

Correlations between Conflict and Racial Identity

(n = 119)

DEGREE OF RACIAL IDENTITY	CONFLICT
Black	-0.15*
White	0.29**
Interracial	-0.24**

*p ≤.10 (two-tailed); ** p ≤.01 (two tailed).

Resolution of the Identity Question

Despite the numerous emotional hazards that the men and women of this study had to negotiate on their journey toward a racial identity, the majority (62.2 percent) indicated that they had been able to resolve the question of racial group membership to their own satisfaction (see Table 7). Most had done so after high school. The complexities involved in this task seemed to postpone the integration of partial identifications into a final black, white, or interracial identity configuration until the post-adolescent/young adulthood years. Given that identity is generally more or less consolidated at the close of adolescence (Blos, 1962, Erikson, 1968), the mastery of this important developmental challenge was somewhat delayed in the men and women of this study. As young adults they seemed to feel less compelled to choose between blackness and white-ness. Rather, many of them found ways to embrace and express both parts of their racial heritage.

However, participants remained vulnerable to uncertainties regarding racial group membership. This was not surprising, given the societal and institutional misidentification and, as Peter Blos (1962) explained, "Ego synthesis at the close of adolescence incorporates unresolved (traumatic) remnants of early childhood" (p. 189).

A small number of individuals (16.8 percent) had been unable to find answers to their racial group belonging by the time of the survey. Per-haps they resembled best the picture of the tragic mulatto that had been popularized in the nineteenth century—a person ravaged by conflict and

Table 7

Resolution of Racial Identity Question

(n = 119)

Degree of Resolution of Racial Identity Question	
None	16.8%
Somewhat	21.0
Large Extent	<u>62.2</u>
	100.0%
Time Period of Resolving Racial Identity Question	
Before Grade School	2.0%
During Grade School	7.1
During High School	29.6
After High School (18-21)	44.9
After High School (22-35)	14.3
It was never an issue	<u>2.0</u>
	100.0%

Columns add up to 100% (except where due to rounding error.)

trapped in a racial no-man's-land. Some of these participants expressed hopelessness about resolving their quest for a racial identity as long as society does not recognize their dual racial background. A light-skinned black woman commented, "The question of my racial identity will never be totally resolved. I am both black and white, and I don't think I ever will be able to accept one race over the other." When asked how she would raise an interracial child if she had one, she responded: "I would let them know that they are both black and white. I would not let them throw away one part of themselves. I know children of Irish and Polish culture and they are taught both. With interracial children it should be the same. When I can be both, without anyone holding a grudge against me for being both, that is when I feel I have resolved the question of my racial identity."

This young woman captured the sentiment of many interracial people. The ability for mixed-race people to check all the categories that identify their racial background promises to end their confusion about who they are racially. How they and the rest of the world will adjust to the idea remains to be seen. Most likely, the ability to safeguard civil rights, full political representation, and a fair share of federally funded programs may have a lot to do with how the new ruling will be received by black people. Similarly, whites may want to have assurances that the status quo of the present power structure will not shift too much by changing racial purity stipulations. In turn, the response of blacks and whites will influence whether interracial people will feel safe enough to publicly embrace both parts of their being.

SELF-ESTEEM

The child's knowledge of his or her inner worth is derived from the incorporation of the family and the extended social environment into the intrapsychic self. According to Banks (1985), there are two major aspects to self-esteem. One is the feeling a person has about him- or herself. The other is the influence others exert on these feelings. The two parts function simultaneously and become intertwined as maturation proceeds. Various experiences in their social environment may interfere with self-esteem development in interracial children. Bradshaw (1992) explains:

The development of healthy self-esteem and an integrated sense of self are more complicated for the biracial person than for the uniracial person. The difficulty of natural developmental tasks may be magnified by several factors: The absence of external validation emanating from lack of social acceptance or ambivalent acceptance; the compromised emotional state of the family that may result from social stigmatization, social stress, and difficult family dynamics; the invisibility or absence of biracial role models; and the absence of biracial referents within the family from which to draw a secure sense of identification, belonging and self-identity. (p. 82)

Given these difficulties, in addition to the racial anonymity that the men and women of this study were subjected to, it was quite unexpected that they had significantly higher self-esteem than the norm group they were compared to. One explanation for these findings is that the sample was not representative. Many of the participants came from middle-class backgrounds and/or were found in highly selective and reputable universities. However, two previous researchers, Arnold (1984) and Spivy (1984) also found that the interracial adolescents they studied had above average levels of self-esteem. Therefore, it was important to look for other explanations.

The Black Power movement of the 1960s, which has done a great deal to instill pride in being black, may have been an important factor in these results. It helped uniracial black as well as biracial children to more readily embrace their own as well as their parents' blackness. Another possible reason for the self-esteem elevation is the biological and psychic link to a white parent. Interracial children may incorporate some of the positive social regard that this parent enjoys.

Finally, various coping mechanisms had successfully protected respondents from excessive conflict and may have preserved their self-esteem. The most important of these seemed to be compartmentalizing a public versus a private identity. Also, the devaluing attitudes held by society toward racially mixed people and their parents may have been separated or compartmentalized from those that they harbored for themselves as an individual or toward their parents. Other defensive maneuvers were denial ("I am black" or "I am white," rather than interracial), rationalization ("I can't be interracial since it is not a legitimate racial category"), and sublimation through high educational and professional achievements. Avoidance was utilized by a few participants with strong white identities, who as a result of traumatic experiences with whites— that is, racism—had abandoned their white identities and white social circles to immerse themselves in the more accepting black world. Conversely, respondents with white identities stayed away from the black community where their racial self-perceptions would come under fire.

Participants who felt ravaged by conflict and uncertainties about racial group membership had significantly lower self-esteem. (Conflict emerged as the most salient predictor of low self-esteem in the hierarchical regression analysis.) Thus the concern of various social scientists (Jacobs, 1977; Payne, 1977; Piskacek and Golub, 1973; Porter, 1971) that conflict about racial group membership jeopardizes the formation of positive self-esteem may be well founded.

Whether or not participants were subjected to racism also played an important role in how they felt about themselves. Racism from blacks diminished both their identification with them and their self-esteem. Racial bigotry from whites, in contrast, pushed them toward their black roots. Individuals who strongly identified with their black parent and the black experience or had the physical appearance of a black person seemed especially deeply pained and upset by such bigotry. "It's like being rejected by your own people," one young man explained.

TREATMENT OF RACIAL IDENTITY ISSUES IN PSYCHOTHERAPY

Interracial people have the same interpersonal and intrapsychic diffi-culties as racially homogeneous people. Therefore, the therapist should not automatically assume that the mixed-race person who seeks psycho-therapy has entered treatment because of identity issues. Racial issues are but one factor in their individual development. Therefore, careful assessment is needed to determine the nature of problems as well as the treatment course.

Racial identity problems may sometimes be masked by symptoms of depression, social isolation, detachment, substance abuse, etc. It is im-portant for the therapist to consider that possibility. If racial identity problems emerge, the therapist should examine the client's own racial self-perceptions. Identifications with significant black or white family members or other role models should be explored. Focusing on certain experiences in the environment may crystallize socially imposed versus actual racial self-perceptions. For instance, growing up in a predomi-nantly black or white community may have taught the client that they can't be interracial. The therapist may question the validity of such an assumption. Is the client able to cope with societal expectations that they deny their whiteness in favor of blackness? Does he or she embrace a public black and private interracial or white identity and is this a com-fortable way of coping with discrepant internal and external messages? Or would he/she rather be out of the closet with his/her unrecognized identity, at least in situations judged to be safe from negative repercus-sions? Is his or her physical appearance compatible with his or her racial identity? For instance, a client with black racial features may be in denial about the difficulty of crossing over into the white world. The therapist needs to address such unrealistic expectations. If the client is in the midst of an identity crisis, which may have been triggered by an entry into a new community, school, college, workplace, or marriage, the therapist should help the client work through the anxiety, confusion, and emo-tional turmoil associated with the crisis and stabilize his or her feelings of racial group belonging.

Because race is a highly emotional and sensitive topic in this country, racial differences between therapist and patient need to be addressed and worked through. If the therapist is white, the interracial patient may wonder about the therapist's understanding of their experiences or racist attitudes directed against them, and therefore omit important information about their concerns and dynamics. With a black therapist they may fear rejection or not being liked unless they show that they have negated their white roots. Therefore, the exploration of the patient's true self-perceptions becomes short-circuited. The therapist should also examine his or her conscious or unconscious biases so that they will not be projected onto the patient and undermine the treatment process.

Ultimately, treatment of racial identity issues should consist of an in-depth exploration of the client's self-perceptions and the encouragement of self-acceptance, even if his or her identity deviates from the norm.

CHAPTER 5

When the Clothes Don't Fit

In the mid 1890s, an "octoroon" (one-eighth black, seven-eighths white) by the name of Homer Plessey was arrested after he challenged a train conductor's refusal to let him have a seat in the all-white car of a train. Plessey took legal action, confronting the patterns of social and legal segregation that had prevailed since slavery, primarily, but not exclusively, in the South. Plessey lost the case in 1896, when the U.S. Supreme Court pronounced such separations consonant with the Fourteenth Amendment in *Plessey vs. Ferguson* (Lofgren, 1987). Although the ruling was supposedly designed to assure the "equality" between blacks and whites, it failed to do so. The fact that a person whose racial background was for the most part white was automatically considered black under the "one drop of black blood" rule highlights the racism underlying these laws. The irrationality underlying this ruling is further emphasized by the fact that Plessey would have been considered white in some states and black in others, depending on each state's interpretation of the law as to who is and is not black.

"Jim Crow," the South's state-approved system of racial segregation, was met with indifference and sometimes even openly endorsed by the federal government. By legally segregating black members of the armed forces and the civil service at various times, the federal government took part in its own version of Jim Crow (Franklin, 1980). Under these laws, blacks became like a group of American untouchables, systematically separated from the rest of the population. The courts paid little attention to the *de jure* racial egalitarianism that was behind the writings of the Fourteenth and Fifteenth amendments. Open legal support from both state and federal government to the American caste system continued for most of the twentieth century (Lombardo, 1988). It was finally challenged after the Second World War. In 1954, in *Brown vs. Board of Education*, the Supreme Court repudiated the separate-but-equal doctrine (Diamond and Cottrol, 1983). After this landmark ruling, a major attack on segregation began. The great numbers of civil rights cases that have been introduced in the federal courts since are witnesses to this fact. However, the "one drop of black blood" rule remained intact, despite renewed efforts to seek its demise. More specifically, in 1983 Susie Guillory Phipps challenged the rule once again in the Louisiana courts. She had been refused a passport after she had defined herself as white on her passport application. On her birth certificate the midwife who had known her family for some time had marked black, although she and her family looked white and some of them were blue-eyed and blond. At the time Louisiana laws held that anyone with more than one-thirty-second black blood would be considered black. After reviewing Phipps's case, the state court ruled that her parents were thirty-seconds black. Therefore, she and her siblings would be classified as black. Phipps took her case to the Louisiana Supreme Court and later to the U.S. Supreme Court. Both courts declined to review the lower court's decision. Therefore, the American tradition to classify anyone with a trace of black blood as black was once more validated. According to Davis (1991), America is the only country in the world that categorizes people by proportion of black blood.

Against this background, the rigidity of the American system of racial classifications, which does not allow interracial people to define themselves by their dual racial background, becomes somewhat easier to understand. State-supported discrimination required racial classification. The law could not separate what it failed to categorize. Tracing black ancestry back as far as possible became a prerequisite to the smooth functioning of the caste system. The idea that a trace of black blood made one black, with all the accompanying disabilities of that status, found widespread acceptance in the United States in black, white, and interracial populations. With the interracial baby boom that occurred after the demise of antimiscegenation laws in 1967, the social and legal invisibility of biracial children and its consequences became increasingly apparent to those concerned with their well-being. Mental health professionals and social scientists (Arnold, 1984; Funderburg, 1994; Jacobs, 1977; Poussaint, 1984; etc.) began to study interracial children and concluded that the "one drop of black blood" rule undermines their ability to form clear racial identities.

Racial status laws had a powerful impact on the emotional well-being of the young people who participated in this study. It forced them into a box that can only accommodate half of who they are. Numerous other problems were attributed to these laws: "As long as I have to choose between being black or white I will have identity problems." "Every time I have to fill out a form I am confronted with the fact that there is no category for me. It's like I don't exist." "It feels like I am choosing my father over my mother, and I don't want to be put into that situation." "If there were an interracial category, I would not have wasted all the energy that I did waste, trying to figure out who I was. At this point I have no more energy left to make myself one ethnicity. I can only be interracial."

Having to define oneself as "other" on census or other official forms also seemed to be unacceptable. It increased the sense of being marginal, an unseen minority, and was frequently viewed as degrading and dehumanizing. "What's an 'other'? Someone from outer space?" exclaimed one young woman during the interview. "I don't think so. I grew up here, I work here and I pay my taxes. Why should I see myself as an 'other'?" A few participants indicated that they write down that they are a "human being." The "human" identity to them seemed preferable to not being able to fully define themselves. Others seemed to reject the whole notion of race. One young man explained, "I don't look at anyone in terms of race. I try to look past that. I like for people to just think of me as who I am. I like to be looked at as a person, friend, etc. Race was not an issue for my parents; otherwise they would not have married. They saw each other as people."

As Table 8 suggests, the more participants felt influenced by racial status laws, the more they felt pressured to define themselves as black and the more significant their conflicts about racial identity. Thus these laws played a powerful role in pushing participants toward blackness and disregarding the other half of their racial makeup. Ultimately, it pressured them toward identity restriction rather than into expansion and integration of the identity configuration.

Pressures to become black differed on the two sides of the racial fence.

Table 8

Influence of Racial Status Laws

(n = 119)

Measure	Influence (%)
None	27.7
Somewhat	37.0
To Large Extend	34.0
Not Sure	.8

Column adds to 100% (except where due to a rounding error)

George, a college senior, explained, "Whites don't differentiate between black and interracial, while blacks will go through all sorts of trouble in convincing you that you are black. They just ignore that you are half white. Interracial people really get mad about that." Openly embracing the unrecognized or, in some instances, the illegitimate white identity rendered them vulnerable to expressions of hostility, ridicule, and even ostracism—especially from blacks who tend to view such identities as a betrayal.

PHYSICAL CHARACTERISTICS

Pettigrew in 1964 challenged the widespread fear in America that racial mixing would result in an "inundation by a black sea." He pointed out the fallacy of that thinking and suggested that if complete random mixing were to occur, the darker skin colors would virtually disappear. The white majority would inundate the black minority, not the other way around. The findings of this study concurred with Pettigrew's observation. As mentioned earlier, the racial appearance or phenotype of participants ranged from medium-brown-skinned people to white-looking people (see chapter 2 for details).

Sharing the phenotype of a given racial group facilitated identification with that group. The more participants had the appearance of a black person, the stronger their black and the weaker their white identities tended to be.[1] Darker-looking participants were less plagued by curious stares or inquiries regarding their racial group membership. Because they were more readily identified as a black person by the outside world and taken for granted as "one of us" by uniracial blacks, their black identity seemed to be more consistently reinforced. Thus adjustment to a world that viewed them as black may have been easier for them than for their lighter-skinned counterparts. For white-looking participants, however, tremendous perceptual and emotional adjustments were required to convince themselves and sometimes the outside world that they were black. Often their struggle to reconcile discrepant physical and social realities led to private solutions. A nineteen-year-old college woman who looked Northern European (fair skin, straight, light brown hair, and green eyes) recalled, "From age five to fifteen I was very confused. I didn't know who I was or how to categorize myself. I would talk to my father about my confusion. He would tell me that I was black. So that didn't help, because when I looked in the mirror, I couldn't agree with him. I finally grew out of it. I decided that I was me, that I was neither black nor white, but interracial." In some instances, there seemed to be attempts to adjust discrepant physical characteristics and societal racial labeling. Some tried to pass as white. Others dated, married, or planned to marry a darker-skinned person to compensate for their own lack of blackness and to be more readily recognized as a black person.

PASSING AS WHITE—OR AS BLACK

Because crossing racial boundaries was a clandestine activity, not much is known about it. Robert Stuckard (1958) estimated that passing involved about three thousand people per year in the decades after slavery. This figure, according to Stuckard, rose to five thousand each year from 1891 to 1910. Eventually it went up to fifteen thousand per year from 1941 to 1950. These numbers, however, are doubtful. The dramatic historical accounts about racially mixed people who crossed the color line into the white world were exaggerated, perhaps because of the terrible anxiety that some whites had about waking up one morning and discovering that the person that they had spent the night with was after all not really white. What is more certain is that the majority of those who passed were men and that it was mainly an urban phenomenon. Men enjoyed greater mobility, and a rural area could not provide the anonymity they needed to live under a "false" racial identity (Spickard, 1992).

Since trying to pass as white continues to be an illegitimate activity for interracial people, there seemed to be apprehension among the men

Table 9
"Passing" as White
(n = 119)

Time Period	Frequently	Sometimes	Rarely	Never	Not Sure/ NA
Thoughts about "Passing" as White in <u>Past</u>	16%	10.9%	17.6%	55.5%	----
Thoughts about "Passing" as White in <u>Present</u>	6.7	5.9	5.9	81.5	----
Actual Attempts to "Pass" as White <u>Past and Present</u>	9.2	11.8	8.4	63.0	7.6

Rows add up to 100% (except where due to a rounding error.)

and women of this study to reveal such intentions. As Table 9 demonstrates, passing behavior seems by no means an event of the past. Apparently, the social and economic privileges associated with whiteness will continue for some to outweigh the danger associated with assuming a "fraudulent" identity.

Participants with white identities, or people with little or no black family or community contact, seemed most preoccupied with crossing racial lines. A nineteen-year-old light-brown-skinned woman with large brown curls admitted, "I used to try to pass—and I did. I would tell others that I was Jewish or Israeli. I would tell my father [black] not to meet me. Later I would feel really guilty for betraying him."

The cost of passing was high. It involved denying family members and friends, uprooting from where the person grew up, and living in constant fear that the deception would be discovered. In many instances these dramatic consequences served as a deterrent to crossing the racial divide. Participants who could but did not want to pass as white constantly felt pressured to tell people that they were "not really white." Coming out of the closet with their blackness, however, frequently elic-

Table 10

Participants Encouraged to "Pass" as White

Within Family

(n = 119)

Response	YES	N0	NA/DK
Relationship			
Father	10.1%	79%	10.9%
Mother	18.5%	74.8%	6.7%
Paternal Grandparents	2.5%	70.6%	26.9%
Maternal Grandparents	6.7%	70.6%	22.7%

Rows add up to 100% (except where due to rounding error).

ited intense anxiety or was perceived as a heavy burden. A twenty-three-year-old development associate, who looked like her blond, blue-eyed, and fair-skinned father, commented, "It's a real hassle to constantly have to explain that I am black and white. It's like opening people's eyes to the big news: 'Hey, I am black.' Yet I would feel real crabby when I got home and I had not said something when a bad joke was made about blacks. It's like coming out of the closet and scary that you might be rejected by the people who all along thought you were white. I want to go to a party and just have fun, not to have to talk about Dr. King."

While the conscious intent to pass seemed to arouse a multitude of uncomfortable feelings, the ability to pass unwittingly seemed welcomed by some of the participants. Such crossing of racial lines helped them take advantage of certain comforts and advantages granted to whites and/or simply enjoy mingling on both sides of the color line without being seen as different. The burden attached to such unintentional passing was a constant preoccupation with if and when they should reveal that they were not white.

A number of participants were encouraged by family members to cross racial boundaries into the white world (see Table 10). Mothers did so with significantly greater frequency than fathers, and maternal grandparents did so significantly more often than paternal grandparents.

The reasons for these differences are not evident from this study. It is quite possible that with the majority of the mothers and grandparents being white, they may have tried to protect their children/grandchildren from the devaluation and hardship that blacks in this white-dominated society must frequently contend with. Their sense of urgency may have been greater in helping their children/grandchildren escape the adversities associated with blackness in America than it would be for a black parent who had had to learn to cope with such experiences from early childhood. In some instances, however, the child's blackness was upsetting because it devalued them as well as their child in the white world.

Interestingly, the impact of "passing" messages was different when it originated from mothers rather than fathers. When mothers told participants that they were white, the white identity predominated and conflict was significantly increased. In contrast, when fathers encouraged interviewees to pass, neither identity nor conflict levels were affected. The underlying reasons for the difference is not readily apparent. It seems that the encouragement to cross racial divides by a black parent was heard as a wish for a better life, while the same message from a white parent was often interpreted by the child as meaning that their blackness was bad or offensive. Helen, a twenty-two-year-old college student with light-brown skin, long curly sandy-colored hair, and a beautiful expressive face, grew up in a racist and dysfunctional family. She spoke poignantly about the feelings of rejection, anger, hurt, and confusion she experienced as a result of her mother's efforts to make her pass as white.

I think my mother really freaked out when I was born and there was this little black child instead of a little Heidi-looking child. She did everything she could to make me look like she looks—blond hair, long straight nose. She always made me as white as possible, so she could identify with me. She was quite subtle about it. She tried to repress anything in me that was culturally black or that was physically black. I was a good child when I was acting white and a bad child when I was acting black. She would straighten my hair every six weeks religiously. . . . I remember one day she had just finished doing my hair and it frizzed [after playing with a water hose]. She yelled at me, how horrible I looked. She was ashamed that I was her daughter. How could I be seen in public with my hair frizzed.

Some light-skinned participants struggled to pass as black. A nineteen-year-old fair-skinned student with brown wavy long hair and hazel eyes explained, "For me it was never a question of passing as white. It was much more of a struggle for my white friends to accept me as black. It has become almost like a crusade that I let people know during the course of our conversation that I am black." Other white-looking respondents seemingly wanted their dual racial background recognized. A twenty-two-year-old woman, who had long blond frizzy hair, green eyes, and fair skin said, "I look so white so I would have to pass as black. When I was young, especially during grade school, I felt I had to prove to black children that I was both black and white. But they had a problem with that."

Not only blacks, but also mixed-race people at times express disdain for those who seek public recognition of their biracial makeup. Claudine Chiawei O'Hearn wrote, "I sneered at those byproducts of miscegenation who chose to identify as mixed, not black. I thought it wishy-washy, an act of flagrant assimilation, treason, passing even" (p. 15).

Thus society's need to categorize people as either black or white regardless of their phenotype has been a bewildering experience—especially for those whose appearance is white. The parents trying to convince a white-looking child that he or she is black defies good parenting, which is based on love, caring, support, respect, and truthfulness. It is difficult to argue with a child who points to his or her white-looking skin and asks, "Mommy how can you tell me I am black when my skin is white?" Not acknowledging both sides of such a child's racial background can be a constant source of frustration and pain for the child as well as for the parent. Of course, the resistance of a given parent to conditioning their child toward blackness may also be due to the wish to protect the child from the hardships associated with the black status. Finally, some white parents may want to validate their biological and psychological connection to the child, which is wiped out with the provision of a black label. It is little wonder that the fight of mixed-race families to gain recognition for their children's dual racial heritage has been a fierce one.

GENDER

Many American black women are unhappy with the way they look and share the fantasy of being white (Russell, Wilson and Hall, 1992). For this society, the beauty ideal continues to be white, although the election of several black Miss Americas signifies a shift in this pattern.

The devaluation of blackness also affects interracial women. Their wish to be white and the hatred that they feel toward their blackness can be pervasive. Helen related, "I always asked people 'What do I look like?' What do I look like?' If they told me I looked black, I was very depressed. If they told me I looked white, I would be very happy. I could never get a handle on my self-image. My first impulse was to compare myself to Christie Brinkley, a white woman with blond hair and blue eyes. In my most white-identified moments, I would come across a black fashion model; I would linger over it at least twenty minutes and dissect everything about it. It was just so rare that I got positive feedback. Everything that was feminine was white, blond, and shorter than me. Everything that I wasn't was feminine."

The women of this study not only tended to have conflicts about racial group membership but also had significantly lower self-esteem than the men. Those with white mothers tended to have lower self-esteem than those with black mothers. With fifty-one of the seventy female respondents having white mothers, the majority of the women's model of identification was a mother whose racial characteristics such as hair texture and skin color may have had higher social regard than their own. In addition, the mother's appearance was often (but not always) pronouncedly different from the daughter's. Consequently, the wish to be like mother was more difficult to fulfill. Helen poignantly spoke about this problem, "I was always confused growing up, I didn't know who I was because I wanted to look like my 'mom.' When I stood on line in the supermarket, the cashier would say to my mother: 'May I help you?' and then say 'May I help you?' to me, like I was not connected to her even though I wanted so much to be. I was always getting social feedback that my mother and I were fundamentally different. So I could not be secure about anything, not knowing what I was racially. I mean if you can't understand yourself outwardly, you can't even begin to understand yourself inwardly." The emotional turmoil about the racial difference between mother and daughter was at times compounded by reaction of the outside world. A young woman who had described her relationship with her mother as "excellent," remembered, "There were difficulties between my mom and me—always being stared at. I used to wish that people just thought that we belonged together. I almost felt guilty for bringing stares upon her. Once we stopped at a restaurant on our way to Ohio to visit my grandfather. When we walked into a restaurant people dropped their knives and forks and just started staring. I was so uncomfortable and felt so bad for my mom. Another time a man passed by and told my mom: 'Oh these nigger babies look real cute when they are small.' My mom always protected me and brushed off racism, but it didn't always work."

Given the fact that many of the participants indicated that they had "good" or "excellent" relationships with their mothers, it is reasonable to assume that many of the white mothers may have been aware of their daughters' struggles. Various supportive measures, such as open discussions, empathy, validation of a child's feelings and assurances of a little girl's attractiveness may have been used by these mothers to ameliorate the conflicts of their daughters. However, these supports may have been insufficient to counteract the disparaging societal messages regarding blackness.

NOTE

1. A positive trend was found between black physical characteristics and black identity. A negative but weakened nonsignificant correlation existed between degree of blackness and white identity. However, these variables did not emerge as salient predictors of identity in the multivaried data analysis (see Appendix B for details).

CHAPTER 6

The Family

MARRIAGE OUTSIDE THE COLOR LINE

Various social pressures continue to impinge on racially mixed couples, despite the legal sanction of such marriages provided by the United States Supreme Court more than thirty years ago. They may struggle to cope with the personal and social aspects of their interracial marriage, and therefore the marriage or they themselves may be under considerable strain. The white members' social status has been diminished as a result of marrying someone black. While they may enjoy social and psychological rewards associated with whiteness when they are alone, as members of a minority-status family their value may be compromised. Similarly, the black partners' status may be in disrepute within the black community for marrying outside of their race. They may be viewed as traitors and treated with anger and contempt. Society at large may view the interracial couple as strange, deviant, or pathological. In many instances the mixed couple may have to find their social life in a community away from their families and away from the neighborhoods in which they grew up. They may experience social isolation and difficulties in finding appropriate housing or employment. Depending on the severity of the stress, their coping skills and available support systems, their own sense of well-being as well as that of their children may be affected.

Interracial children may become aware that their families are not viewed with the same regard and respect as other children's families. They may witness racist abuses of their black parent or traumatic devaluation of their white parent. A thirty-four-year-old professional woman became quite emotional when she recalled overhearing two white nurses talking about her mother: "She must be a whore for sleeping with a black guy and having a black child." The mother was a physician at the hospital.

Since young children more or less view themselves as an extension of their parents, social devaluation of their parents can be taken quite personally. Intense hurt, anger, shame, and humiliation can be experienced as a result. With the parental ideal blemished, the internalization of a socially devalued parent results in hate and subsequent feeling of guilt about the hate. Thus the psychological quest for an ideal becomes more difficult (Kardiner and Ovesey, 1962).

FAMILY STRUCTURE

Like uniracial children, interracial children may be found in various types of living arrangements and family configurations. They may live in intact families, with adoptive parents, in single-parent households, or in blended families. They may also have white mothers and black fathers or black mothers and white fathers. In case of blended families, the biological and stepparent may be either black or white, and they may have uniracial white or black siblings. (For demographic details of the participants see Appendix A.)

While family structure has important implications for family interaction and the development of all children, it may have a particularly strong impact on interracial children. For instance, children living in a single-parent household may be deprived of access to the culture and values of the nonresident parent. Since interracial children are expected to assume the racial identity of their black parent, the absence or limited contact with that parent can present a major problem. An eighteen-year-old economics major, who was raised by his white mother after his black father abandoned him when he was six months old, commented, "I always knew that I was biracial, but I always denied my black identity. I denied it because I did not know it existed."

In the case of remarriage, the race of the new partner may influence whether the child's blackness, whiteness, or interracialness is stressed. Remarriage may also change the racial balance in the family so that the interracial child is the only person of color, or the only person who represents whiteness. Parental dynamics and attitudes may be influenced by these factors. A white stepparent and/or their relatives may regard the child's blackness as a stigma to the family, while a black stepparent and/or extended family member may view the child's whiteness as a symbol of betrayal to their race. As a result, the child might not be fully accepted. He or she may be subjected to racist remarks or may be pressured consciously or unconsciously by either immediate or extended family members toward being more white or more black. The child usually feels upset, hurt, and rejected by such pressures. Sidney (see chapter 1) recalled bitterly, "My stepfather's parents [white] would speak of 'niggers' and then look at me and say 'oh sorry.' I don't care if I ever see them again. I never felt accepted by them. My mother would try not to make me look so black, so that they would accept me. But that really didn't help."

In some families, marital conflict and siblings rivalries between monoracial and interracial siblings may be played out along racial and color lines. Sidney's relationship with her white half sister was fraught with turmoil until she left for college. She recalled, "There used to be a lot of jealousy between us. She got so much attention and I just could not deal with it. I was constantly asked 'Why can't you be like her?' which was really awful for me. She was accepted and I wasn't, so everything was really difficult for me."

Differences in racial appearance among siblings can place a heavy burden on their relationship. Sidney explained that her grandparents idealized her blond and blue-eyed half brother and sister, while she felt barely tolerated. Her sister especially seemed to feel badly and guilty about the preferential treatment. Sometimes the darkness of one sibling prevents another one from acting upon his or her ability or wish to cross over into the white world. The brother or sister who is unable to pass may experience jealousy and resentment as well as guilt. A young retail clerk who had the physical appearance of a medium-dark-skinned black woman remembered, "When I was eight years old, my brother went to visit my father. My brother is very light. He can pass. When I stepped forward to say good-bye to him, the bus driver said to my mother: 'I don't want him on my bus; I don't want to baby-sit for "nigger babies."' I remember feeling real bad for him and for myself. My brother wants to pass. He straightens his hair so he can, but if they know that I am his sister, they know that he is black too." Siblings who can pass may feel relief and at the same time guilt for having access to privileges that their darker brother or sister may be deprived of.

GETTING TOGETHER

Few interracial children in the 1930s, '40s and '50s, when interracial marriage was illegal in many parts of this country, had contact or ever enjoyed close relationships with their white grandparents (Roberts, 1983). Until fairly recently, interracial unions usually occurred surreptitiously. Golden (1954), who interviewed fifty black/white families in Philadelphia, found that racially mixed couples frequently had to conceal their courtship. They had quiet weddings, eloped, or hid their marriage from coworkers and employers. Even after the last twelve states abolished laws against racially mixed marriages, the opposition against such unions continued. Ernest Porterfield (1978) found that 65 percent of the forty interracial families he studied were rejected by their white relatives and only 27.5 percent by their black relatives. With black families being more receptive to mixed-race families, interracial children were more likely to be centered in the black family.

Contrary to expectations, the opposite pattern occurred with the men and women of this study. They had significantly more contact with the white than the black family. The reasons for these findings are not quite clear, but it is reasonable to assume that the prevalence of the white wife/black husband marital pattern in conjunction with the fathers rarely being the residential parent of their children in a separation or divorce played an important role. The majority (79.9 percent) of the participants had white mothers, and only 5 percent of the mothers who were divorced or separated from their spouse/partner were nonresidential parents. There were certainly exceptions to this pattern, in which white mothers, unable to cope with family or social pressures evoked by their interracial relationships, abandoned their children and the black father assumed the responsibility of caring for the child. Or the white father left, and the black mother raised the child.

The degree of contact participants had with either side of the family had important implications for their psychosocial adjustment. When contact was mostly restricted to the white family, participants tended to identify with them and had greater difficulties in adapting to a world that regarded them as black. A twenty-six-year-old white-looking truck driver, Charles, who grew up with his white mother after his father died, explained in a troubled voice, "No, I have no identity. I don't have a grasp of whether I am white or black. I am not comfortable with myself." The resistance to owning their blackness became intensified if participants were raised in a white community where they identified with the people who lived there and where they internalized racist messages against blacks. One fair-skinned young woman was in and out of the closet with her blackness. She had been adopted by two white professionals and grew up in an affluent white community. Because she looked white, her blackness was a secret that she only revealed to close and trusted friends. The few participants who grew up with mostly black family members had strong black identities and reported minimal conflict about racial group membership. However, they seemed to long to be in touch with the white side of their racial heritage and their white parent. Thus restriction of contact to either the black or the white side of the family led to emotional difficulties.

The presence of interracial siblings could ameliorate these problems. Often they served as an important source of biracial identifications and as models in coping with confusing racial group membership questions. An eighteen-year-old high school senior commented, "My parents would tell me to see myself as completely black. That was giving me doubts. I consider myself interracial. I did not want to lean to one side. My sisters and brothers see themselves as interracial and they agree that I am interracial too. My father especially pushes me to see myself as black. But I guess he is trying to keep me from getting hurt."

Acceptance

Overall, participants described their parents as loving, committed, and sensitive to their needs. A college student, when asked about the most important experience or person(s) that influenced how he saw himself racially, responded, "My family—the amount of affection and support they have shown me, being there, making me feel loved." A twenty-eight-year-old woman who grew up in a black community where she was harassed by other children for having a white mother said, "I would not hide my mother. She was a good mother, made cookies, went to PTA meetings, covered up for me if I was late. So I would not hide her."

The black and white extended family members were seen by study participants as similar in acceptance. This view changed for the immediate family. Participants tended to have a better relationship with white than black family members (for details, see Tables 11 and 12). While the responses of the men and women did not offer a good understanding of

Table 11

Quality of Relationships with Black and White*

Immediate Family members

(n=119)

Quality of Relationship	Mean	SD	Paired t-test
Black Member	11.05	7.95	-1.94
White Member	13.71	9.05	(p ≤ .10)

*Measured as continuous variable.

the underlying reason for these findings, one can speculate that they were related to the race of the primary caretaker. With the majority of the participants having white mothers and with mothers being frequently the primary caretaker of children when a couple breaks up, the connectedness to the white parent may often have been greater than to the black parent. It is also possible that the societal devaluation of the black parent may have influenced the parent/child relationship. The child may consciously or unconsciously blame the black parent for his or her own hardships encountered as a person of color or may devalue the parent because of the racist messages he or she may have incorporated within a racist society. Finally, the pressure to assume a black identity, which generally tended to come from the black parent, was resented by some participants.

A rather surprising picture evolved with the extended family (see Table 12). Overall, the white extended family seemed as accepting of participants as their black relatives. Given the traditional rejecting stance of white relatives, these finding were quite unexpected. The change in attitudes may be attributed to the abolishment of the antimiscegenation laws in 1967 and increase in contact beween blacks and whites as a result of Civil Rights legislation in the 1960s. These factors may have rendered interracial marriage less alien, and greater familiarity between the two racial groups may have diminished some of the fears and negative stereotypes of each other. However, there were exceptions to this pattern. Helen (discussed in previous chapters) recalled, "My [white] relatives could not really see me as a relative. They were nice, but nice like to a visitor—not as someone of the family. I felt I was a stigma to them." In another case, a mother had abandoned her daughter after her father had threatened to kill her black husband. Having married in secret, she did

Table 12

Acceptance by the Black and White Extended Family (n=119)

Degree of Acceptance	Not at all	Some-what Unaccept.	No Dif-ference	Some what Accepted	Very much	Not Sure
Black Relatives	----	2.5%	6.7%	10.1%	65.1%	15,1%
White Relatives	4.2	9.2	4.2	16.8	65.1	4.2

not let her parents know that her husband was black until her daughter was born. Apparently terrified of her father's violent threats, she returned to Tennessee and never saw her daughter again. The daughter was raised by her father and stepmother.

The arrival of a grandchild could drastically alter the attitude of a family that had rejected the cross-racial marital choice of their child. As Crohn (1995) explained, a grandchild is "their own flesh and blood who will carry on their spirit." They connect past and future generations.

One college senior, whose maternal grandparents had disowned her mother when she married a black man, said:

When I was born, my mother started sending pictures of me to her parents. At first they did not respond, but one day they wrote back and asked her to visit and bring me. I think that meant a lot to my mother. She went and they talked for a long time. Eventually my mother brought my father along, and I guess my grandparents realized that he was a good person, and not any different than they were. Now the whole family accepts us. They want us to visit all the time and they love us to death. So now we have an excellent relationship with them. My grandparents always seem glad to see us.

Rejections were not restricted to white relatives. A thirty-year-old medical secretary explained that her black father was disinherited by his parents because he married a white woman.

While acceptance is generally a conflict-reducing experience, being embraced by black relatives seemed to signal "You are one of us," "You have a home," and "You belong." Acceptance by black relatives significantly increased identification with them and diminished conflict about racial group membership.

Acceptance by the white family seemed to encourage high self-esteem. Such receptiveness seemed to have emphasized the link to a socially, psychologically, and economically privileged racial group. It also signified that they were embraced as a total person, whose blackness was not perceived as bad or negative and/or did not represent a barrier to a loving and supportive relationship.

EXPOSURE TO CULTURE

With white culture the most prominent one within American institutions and mass media, it was hardly surprising that the mainstream experience predominated for the men and women of this study (for details, see Table 13). Many participants were raised in predominantly white or racially integrated communities where white culture was an integral part of life. One unexpected finding was the significantly greater participation in white than in black social gatherings. Again, this may be partly related to the high number of white mothers who became custodial parents in case of divorce or separation and the child then being centered in the white rather than in the black family system. Also, the greater acceptance of interracial children in recent years by their white relatives may account for these findings.

The more interracial children were immersed in white cultural life, the more they identified with it, but because this was a "forbidden" identity, they experienced significant emotional turmoil. Conversely, the more frequent their contact with black culture, the stronger their black identities and the less conflict they suffered about who they were racially.

The frequency of exposure to black literature and historical and political issues suggests that the families of participants made special efforts to make black culture part of their lives. Such exposure acted as a powerful antidote against negative stereotypes associated with blackness. A twenty-one-year-old student who grew up in an all-white community explained:

When you are not exposed to black culture, you may see your blackness as negative, as bad. You may associate blackness with crime, low test scores, and broken families. But when you are exposed to black culture, you learn that blacks are not only good in sports. It allows you to take your blackness and transform it from a source of insecurity and shame to a source of pride. You only have conflict when you are not comfortable with part of yourself. When you are exposed to both cultures, you can be proud of both and be both.

Table 13

Number of Participants Being Exposed to Black and White Culture

Within the Family (in Percent)

(n = 119)

Frequency:	Almost Never		Sometimes		Often		Almost All theTime	
Culture:	Black	White	Black	White	Black	White	Black	White
Social Gatherings	21.8	4.2	32.8	10.9	30.3	37.8	15.0	147.1
Food	33.6	----	31.9	12.6	26.1	34.5	8.4	52.9
Church	68.1	40.3	21.8	21.8	7.6	10.9	2.5	26.9
Music	7.6	4.2	20.2	23.5	33.6	34.5	38.7	37.8
Literature	19.3	1.7	44.5	13.4	26.9	30.3	9.2	54.6
Television	9.2	.8	52.9	6.7	29.4	37.0	8.4	55.5
Discussions of Historical and Political Issues	21.8	13.4	34.5	39.5	33.6	37.0	10.1	10.1

Black and White Exposure Items in Rows add up to 100% (except where due to rounding errors).

RACIAL LABELING

Interracial parents have been caught in a no-win situation when their child begins to ask questions about racial group membership. If they emphasize blackness, they clash with the reality of their child's dual genetic racial makeup and/or interracial identity. On the other hand, an interracial label may not be congruent with society's view of the child. Finally, a white racial label would be challenging a major taboo and often

Table 14

Black and Interracial Labeling in the Family*

(n = 119)

Type of Label	Mean	SD	Paired t-test
Black	38.73	47.88	-1.67
Interracial	51.04	46.40	(p ≤ .10)

*Measured as continuous variable.

is not in harmony with the child's phenotype. Consequently, no matter which racial label the parents provide, they may inadvertently set the stage for conflict from early childhood on.

In the past, interracial parents have tried to protect their children from assuming the "wrong" identity by conditioning them towards blackness. Baptiste (1985), however, observed that contemporary interracial parents stress both parts of their children's racial heritage. This observation was only partly confirmed by the accounts of the men and women of this study. As Tables 14 and 15 illustrate, while more families tended to emphasize the biracial than the black background of their children, black racial labeling was not an event of the past. Similarly, while the white label was by no means passé, it was the least common one.

The message communicated to study participants about racial group membership played an important role in their racial self-perceptions. More specifically, black, white, and interracial labels emerged as the most salient predictors of the corresponding racial identities.[1] Some caution is warranted when interpreting these findings. Sometimes respondents did not immediately recall what family members communicated to them about their racial group, but after some probing, they usually did reply. It is possible, therefore, that their answers have been in part a projection of how they saw themselves rather than what family members communicated to them about racial group membership.

Several reasons may underlie the significant relationship between racial labeling and racial identity. In absence of a socially recognized interracial category, interracial parents are expected to prepare their children for the reality that their interracial heritage may not be recognized by society at large. Therefore racial labeling, especially black racial labeling, is often done on a more conscious, deliberate, and frequent level

Table 15

Black and White Labeling in the Family*

(n = 119)

Type of Label	Mean	SD	Paired t-test
Black	38.73	47.88	6.87
White	5.75	13.25	(p ≤ .01)

*Measured as continuous variable.

than in families with uniracial black or white children. Similarly, some parents focus on the interracialness of their children in an effort to counteract societal misidentification of their children. Such labeling may occur directly, or it may occur indirectly through a failure to challenge the child's interracial self-perceptions.

As the findings of the study showed, the racial background of the parent plays an important role in what racial label they provide. Thus, black family members tended to emphasize blackness, while a significant number of white family members stress the interracial background. The reasons for difference in racial labeling approaches are not clear from the results. One could speculate that blacks have a deeper understanding of the negative repercussions of denying one's black roots. By stressing the child's blackness in favor of whiteness, they may want to spare their children pain. White parents, not having suffered the toxins of racism, may feel more at liberty to encourage their child to embrace both parts of their racial background. Also, some may be reluctant to provide a racial label that denies their parenthood and existence.

As the accounts of study participants revealed, some parents seem influenced by their own beliefs in what they communicate about racial group belonging, others by external forces or the physical appearance of their child.

A twenty-three-year-old electrician related, "My mother saw me initially as black, because I saw myself as black. But as I grew older, I saw myself as interracial, so her perception changed. She realized I was interracial, not just black. My father also saw me initially as black, but as I grew older he agreed that I was interracial." Another young man who resembled his white mother commented, "My mother has said I could pass as white. She didn't think it would be a problem. At this point, however, she thinks that less, because my hair used to be much straighter and my mouth is more full now."

The messages that various family members conveyed to study participants about racial group membership were not necessarily in harmony. A nineteen-year-old daughter of a white mother and a black father explained, "My mother makes the point that I am interracial, contradicting my father if he insists that I am black. He tells me that the world will see me as black—not as interracial. During Black History Month, he especially emphasizes my blackness. My brother and I discussed the issue of our race and we call ourselves the 'golden children.'" A nineteen-year-old fair-skinned housewife, who defined herself as black in the predominately black community where she grew up, recalled, "My father insisted that I was black. He told me, 'You can't be both black and white. If you are black, you are black.' I knew different, however. I listened to my mother, who told me I was mixed and that is how I feel about myself—as mixed."

Several of the participants indicated that they challenged their parents' attempts to convince them they were black. Although they seemed to understand that their parents were trying to protect them from getting hurt, they felt upset when their parents failed to acknowledge their dual racial heritage. It was the impression of this researcher that such challenging seemed to occur particularly in adolescents.

Bewildered as to how to handle the racial group membership question of their child, some parents avoided the topic altogether or left it up to the child to decide who they wanted to be racially. Such parental silence was interpreted sometimes as encouragement to cross racial boundaries and at other times as permission to embrace an interracial identity. A few respondents said their parents fluctuated between black and white labels. This pattern could reflect a belief that their child was as much white as black, and therefore either label would be appropriate. Or it could signal parental racism and defensive splitting, which was quite toxic to the child. One light-brown-skinned woman recalled, "My mother saw me as black when I was bad and white when I was good. She preferred for my friends to be white and told me to stay out of the sun so I would not get darker. I think she would have preferred for her children to be white."

Instead of race, some parents emphasized the importance of human qualities. This approach left participants frequently ill-equipped to cope with a society that stipulated a black identity. A graduate student related, "You perceive different signals within the family and outside of the family. The family may underplay the issue of race and stress that you should just see yourself as you, while the rest of society sees you as black and may even call you a 'nigger'."

Participants who were consistently told by family members that they were black enjoyed significant conflict reduction. The emotional benefit of black categorization seemed particularly prominent when parents coupled their message with regular exposure to black role models, instilled pride in the black cultural heritage, and prepared the child to cope with racism. Under these circumstances, the child's black identity was not simply based on communications such as "You are black" but was deeply embedded in day-to-day experiences. Consequently, a stable primary black identity, which coincided with the societal perception of the person, could evolve.

Some families, however, pressured participants excessively, especially if they saw signs that their child's racial identity did not concur with the socially prescribed identity. Such pressures seemed to be frequently predicated upon the family's concern that the child would get hurt unless they could get them to assume the "right" identity. For a variety of reasons such demands seemed to be contraindicative to emotional health. Frequently they suffocated the necessary racial identity exploration process. As a result, the child would get stuck with the question, Who am I? A light-skinned orderly, who grew up with a black mother and a black stepfather (he never met his white father) explained:

I never could communicate with my family—really talk to them. I had to make my own rules. Everyone in my family just spoke black—no buts, no questions about it! I am still confused. I am not sure whether I really relate to the black or the white side. I want to blend in. I want to be in the middle and sometimes I wonder if I [will] continue to wonder all my life or whether I am going to make my own path.

It is interesting to note that this young man identified his race at the beginning of the interview as "other," rather than choosing one of the socially and legally recognized racial categories. Another young woman commented, "My grandmother [black] had an important influence on me. She tried to make me forget that I am both races. She pushed that I was black—physically and mentally. The more she pushed, the more I rebelled and saw myself as interracial."

Especially in instances where the white parent was absent, participants were upset when their wish to preserve their whiteness was met with intolerance. Disowning the white identity part seemed equivalent to negating not only half of themselves but also their white parent. A student whose white adoptive parents had raised her in a white community but stressed that she was black said, "I am wondering if I am forgetting about my natural mother's side. I keep on saying I am black, black, black, but how would she feel if I am just totally ignoring the Swedish side of my family. She is not acknowledged when I say I am all black. Should I just forget about that?"

Interracial labeling was unrelated to conflict and frequently occurred on a much less emphatic level than black or white labeling. For instance, some parents simply refrained from challenging the interracial self-perceptions of their child, or incorporated both racial heritages in their lifestyle. A son of a military officer commented, "My mother and father did not emphasize any particular race. It was natural that I was interracial, given who I was and given my interracial identity." Another young man explained, "The environment my parents created taught me that I was interracial. I was brought up in a home that did not completely lean to one side or another. My parents were open to my own development. I liked it that way. It was good for me."

Participants who were constantly exposed to white racial labeling had significant conflict. This was not surprising, since such labeling clashed with societal messages and was in violation of racial status laws. Especially when white family members encouraged the white identity, participants often perceived that their blackness was a stigma to that relative or something to be ashamed of (see chapter 5). Thus the messages family members provided about racial group belonging had major implications in how participants saw and felt about themselves.

NOTE

1. See the Pathdiagram in Appendix B.

CHAPTER 7

Places to Live and Learn

COMMUNITIES

In the past most interracial children grew up within black neighborhoods where their families found protective havens (Adams, 1973; Drake and Cayton, 1945). Social changes that occured during the last few decades may have changed this pattern. The breakdown of racial barriers during the 1960s enabled interracial couples to leave the poverty, neglect, and crime that many black neighborhoods continue to suffer from. Also, with the rise of the Black Power movement, the black community increasingly viewed blacks who married whites as traitors, and the lightness of interracial children no longer put them into a preferred position. Finally, because of the dramatic increase of divorce and illegitimate births during the last few decades, a considerable number of interracial children are being raised by white mothers. These mothers may feel more rooted and comfortable in white or mixed communities.

The findings of this study reflect some of these changes. The majority of the people in this study grew up in white or racially integrated neighborhoods. (The mean number of years spent in white communities was 8.18; polyethnic, 7.97; and black, 3.42. Whether respondents were raised

in a black, white, or racially integrated community affected their adjustment.

White Community: Out of Place

While the white community frequently offered attractive surroundings
and a better education than the black community, many of the participants who grew up there felt traumatized by the experience. Their blackness and their being the offspring of an interracial union often invited
negative attention—racial slurs, taunting, rejection, and at times bodily
harm. A twenty-five-year-old graduate student with reddish-brown
frizzy hair and a light complexion recalled with bitterness:

I had to do a lot of fighting because of prejudice. I was on the offensive all the
time. I was called everything that was black and white: Zebra, vanilla fudge
swirl. Oreo was a big one. I was a little guy. I couldn't fight all of them, although
I tried. Everybody was white. There was no one else I could relate to. No one
had the same experience as me. I saw myself as an ugly kid because people used
to call me ugly. My features were not considered attractive by the other people
in my community. When you are a kid, it really matters when you are different.
I could not just blend in, because I was so different. If they picked on you—
made an issue of your blackness—you could sit there and be passive. You could
become an introvert, but then you were not included. I wanted to be accepted,
so I became an extrovert. I was expected to entertain. But I didn't like to be a
clown, at least not all the time. I was tired of it! I overcompensated and became
a loud and boisterous person. I was critical and opinionated. I attacked before I
could be attacked. That is how I protected myself.

With their blackness inviting abuse, their black roots frequently became a major burden. The adolescent period seemed particularly painful.
Due to the strong taboos against cross-racial dating, many of the study
respondents had never been asked for a date. Similarly, being fearful of
rejections, they often refrained from pursuing potential dating partners.
Being deprived of an important adolescent experience, they felt lonely,
depressed, and plagued by a deep sense that there was something wrong
with them.

Only 7.6 percent of the participants indicated that they would like to
live in a white community if they had a choice. The longer participants
lived in one, the more strongly they identified with whites. These identities seemed not only to be the result of proximity and their awareness
that whites were the dominant racial group in this country but also of a
need to distance themselves from mixed-race roots that were considered

inferior and subjected them to abuse. The interracial identity was found to be significantly diminished in respondents who grew up in white neighborhoods. Embracing a "forbidden" identity and being removed from who they actually were, they experienced significant conflict. The toxin of racism that all too often reared its ugly head added to their emotional turmoil and left deep emotional scars.

Black Community: Being Too White

For a variety of reasons, life in the black neighborhood did not always offer a better experience. Having a white parent and therefore being seen as "not black enough," participants were frequently suspect in regard to racial group allegiance. They often felt tested, subject to caustic and hostile remarks, ostracism, and even physical attack. To cope with these affronts and to dispel doubts about their authenticity as blacks, they frequently tried to hide physical or cultural signs of their whiteness. They adopted African hairstyles, dress, speech, and mannerisms and immersed themselves deeply in black causes. A light-brown-skinned woman related, "I used to be ostracized by other blacks as though I had a disability because I had a white parent. Since I wear dreadlocks, things have changed for the better. It is a sign that I take pride in my African heritage."

Especially women who looked white seemed to encounter anger and jealousy from darker-skinned black women. Monique, a young woman with fair skin and long chestnut-colored hair, said that for a while she could not walk down the street in the black neighborhood where she lived without being subjected to caustic and hostile remarks such as: "Who do you think you are!" "You think you are better?!" "Whitey go home." One woman recalled being attacked as a teenager by a girl who pulled out some of her hair in an effort to establish whether it was real or a wig. The attack had been prompted by the girl's fear that she would lose her boyfriend to the participant.

Consequently, having a white parent and looking white in the black community could be a distinct disadvantage. The longer respondents lived there, the more significantly their self-esteem became diminished. Of course, it is quite feasible that the harsh living conditions that continue to prevail in many black neighborhoods may have been the underlying reasons for low esteem. However, the constant message that something is wrong with you because you have a white parent or that you do not measure up as a black person seemed to powerfully undermine the participants' ability to feel good about themselves. The few respondents (4.2 percent) who preferred black community living had immersed themselves in black cultural life. They had abandoned their interracial and white identification, and/or their white parent was either absent or willing to remain in the background. Thus the popular opinion that the black community presents a haven for interracial children could not be confirmed by the experiences of the men and women of this study.

The Racially Integrated Community: Acceptance

The majority of the participants (83.2 percent) saw the racially mixed community as the most desirable one. The popularity of the integrated neighborhood was related to the greater tolerance for racial differences that characterized them, which translated for many participants into feelings of acceptance of themselves and their families. A fair-skinned woman explained, "I definitely like a mixed neighborhood. There is a lack of stress on race. You don't have to choose sides and be constantly tested. With blacks you always have to prove that you are black enough. With whites you have to worry that they know you are black." Other comments were: "It feels more comfortable. . . . I feel more accepted . . . less stress . . . it includes both sides of my identity . . . it's a healthier environment . . . less prone to prejudices . . . less rigid ideas. . . . I would rather be around people who have been exposed to both sides of the coin. . . . It's more conducive to being a full person."

Growing up in a racially diverse neighborhood was associated with significant reduction in conflict. The freedom to express both black and white identity components without arousing disapproval was welcomed and celebrated by the respondents. Being accepted as who they were, and being able to embrace both black and white culture and friends without arousing disapproval, enhanced their overall psychosocial adjustment. As Spurlock (1986) points out, children who are viewed as "attractive" and "acceptable" by the broader environment are better equipped to cope with adversities that life may present. The polyethnic environment seemed to be such a place for interracial people. Also, the presence of other interracial families reduced their sense of being different, alone, or marginal. Meeting people with similar backgrounds and experiences presented a wonderful opportunity to share and work through some of the hurts inflicted by racial bigotry. It also provided a chance to meet interracial role models. Consequently, a racially integrated community offered many opportunities for participants to flourish and to feel good about themselves and their families.

SCHOOLS

Intolerance for racial differences was even more keenly experienced in the school than in the community at large. The daily interaction with the same group of children did not allow respondents to avoid those who made an issue of their blackness, their whiteness, or their mixed racial heritage. Also, children usually have not learned the euphemisms and restraint that frequently characterize adult communications. The negative stereotypes and prejudices they pick up within their families or society at large are often expressed with devastating directness.

In some schools the administration and teacher's message that racism was not tolerated was clear. They not only confronted racist attitudes directly but also taught cultural sensitivity and coping mechanisms. A twenty-four-year-old customer service agent recalled, "Teachers helped me by being honest. They made me aware that people would always see me as different—that goes for blacks as well as whites—and that I would have to learn to deal with that. They taught me that I did not have to choose to be black or white, that it was up to me. They also helped me to see that race was unimportant, that it was the person that counted." In some other schools, however, teachers were not only ignorant about the special needs of interracial children, but they failed to confront racist abuses.

White Schools

Not enjoying the same social regard and respect as white classmates and lacking interracial or black role models, participants who went to predominately white schools tended to feel bad about themselves. Some suffered from poor body images and longed to be white. A light-brown-skinned black woman who attended white grade and high schools recalled, "I remember times when I was younger, I wanted to be white. I wanted long hair, a different nose, body, etc.—like the people on television. I felt just kind of put together—mixed. I wasn't even like black or white separate, just a different kind of person."

The preconceived notion about mixed-race children and their families that frequently characterizes white schools often weighed heavily on participants. A thirty-five-year-old housewife explained, "The teachers in my school had a low opinion of blacks in general, but they had an even lower opinion of interracial children. They had to have something wrong with their brain because their parents were in a mixed marriage. I was expected to be smarter than the black kids, because of my white parenthood, yet I was excused from knowing some things because it was assumed that I had more problems than blacks or whites."

Some teachers failed to differentiate between black and racially mixed children. Such misidentification could be offensive and upsetting. One young woman remembered, "I was called upon by a teacher to comment on a current events article. The teacher said I was chosen number one for my writing skills, and secondly because I was black. I was extremely insulted by that. But I realized that white people do not necessarily see me as both black and white."

Although participants were seen as racially and culturally different, they frequently were expected to assimilate and act white. These pressures were especially upsetting to those with interracial or black identities. Some respondents fought back and insisted on the recognition of their racial identities. Others complied because they wanted to be accepted and be part of the larger group. The price of such compliance could, however, encourage identity distortion or conflict. Failing to own their blackness, which represented a major part of themselves, or denying their ties to the black side of their families and community, they were often uncomfortable and ill at ease with who they were or where they came from.

Some participants with white identities, or those who tried to cross into the white world, became anxious when their black parent appeared on the scene. Their connection highlighted that they were not white, threatened their social status, and revealed their effort to live a "fraudulent" existence. The resentment toward the black parent for such exposure and for blocking the door to passing often was mixed with feelings of guilt and shame for betraying someone they loved.

Overall, a predominately white school environment was not conducive to the emotional well-being of participants. The message that their families were abnormal or deviant or lacked morals was frequently internalized and encouraged low self-regard. Because such a social milieu failed to instill pride in blackness, identity integration tended to be jeopardized.

Black Schools

Frequently the condition of acceptance in black schools was proof that participants had negated their white roots. Even though many complied with these demands, being half white subjected them to insults and rejections. Epithets like "zebra," "oreo," "light dog," or "salt" and exclusion from gatherings were used to show disapproval. One young woman recalled the humiliation she felt when her classmates refused to eat the cookies her white mother had baked for a school function.

Unable to cope with the harassment, some became socially isolated. A thirty-five-year-old welfare mother remembered, "The black mothers in my school told their kids not to play with us because we had a white mother. After a while it did not bother me too much anymore, because I stayed in the house, read a lot, and listened to music. I always felt if they could not accept my mother, they could not accept me. I was proud to be both black and white, not only proud to be black." Others tried to silence doubts about their blackness by immersing themselves into black ghetto culture or by hiding white family members in order to avoid uncomfortable questions or abuse. One medium-brown-skinned young man remembered riding to school with his white mother and telling his black classmates that she was the car pool lady. He did not want to jeopardize his being viewed as black or "stir the pot."

Black schools played a major role in conditioning participants toward blackness with positive and negative consequences. The consistent message, "you are black" pushed them to ignore their whiteness, facilitated their adaptation to this country's system of racial classification, and offered them a racial home. At the same time, however, it required the denial of a major part of themselves and their family and was therefore upsetting.

Grade school and junior high school seemed to be particularly stressful. Not only did the insistence that they disregard their whiteness invite bafflement, self-questioning, and anxiety in the child, but at this early age they had developed few skills to cope with a world that did not allow them to be interracial. White-looking participants seemed to be especially at risk. Their own confusion about racial group belonging was often mirrored in their social surroundings. A fair-skinned housewife remembered her grade-school years:

I was not sure which race I was, because I was mixed. Some of my friends (they really weren't my friends) said, "She is white." Others said, "No she is black. What are you talking about? I know her father. He is black. Just because her mother is white doesn't mean she is white." I was confused over *what* I was. My close friends didn't care. I let them know that I was mixed. But the ones that would say, "She is white," I would tell them, "No, I am not white, I am black."

The black identity that this young woman eventually developed was not altogether egosyntonic. She remarked at the end of the interview, "I want to learn some things about white people, just as I learned things about black people. I would like to get to feel both sides of me and maybe I would know which side I am comfortable with and get along with."

The low self-esteem scores associated with black grade school attendance suggest that the intense pressure to alter their self-perceptions had an adverse impact on their self-image. Again, it is entirely possible that the conditions of neglect frequently found in black schools also played an important role in these findings. However, being constantly on the defensive about their whiteness and often feeling excluded by the "in crowd" seemed to adversely affect their sense of self-worth.

Racially Integrated Schools

Participants felt less stressed in a multiracial school environment. The greater acceptance of racial differences that were typically found in such social milieus tended to be translated into self-acceptance. Claudette, a young college graduate (see chapter 1), when asked about the most important experiences that influenced her racial identity responded, "School I guess first and then my parents. We had black, white, Israeli, and Indian teachers. I learned from all of them. It contributed to my feeling that it's okay to be different. I felt enriched and broadened by the experience."

However, not all racially integrated schools were free of racial tensions. Intergroup tensions pressured participants to choose sides and created loyalty conflicts. There was a constant concern as to whether they were doing the right thing in regard to their choice of friends. If they had white friends, they felt as though they were betraying their black friends. If they had black friends, they were concerned about being disloyal to their white friends. The pressures were especially intense from the black side. Too frequent association with whites earned them the reputation of being traitors, snobs, or sellouts and invited rejections. A common coping mechanism was to keep friendships with whites low key or clandestine.

Overall, a polyethnic school environment was the most desirable educational milieu for the participants of this study. While it did not spare them from the racial tensions that characterize the rest of this country, it was more conducive to their feeling whole and not lacking in whiteness or blackness.

COLLEGE

For many participants, entry into college did not offer an escape from a world obsessed with race. Rather it catapulted some into a racial identity crisis after they had had just emerged from the identity struggles typical for adolescence. The crisis often started when they were asked to fill out a college application that lacked a racial category reflecting their dual racial background. To conform to social conventions and, in some instances to take advantage of some of the privileges offered to minority students, many respondents identified themselves as black. Having done so, they found that the black college community began reaching out for them, trying to incorporate them into their organizations and social circles. This gesture was welcomed and most beneficial for students with strong black identities, those floundering about who they were racially, or those who felt socially isolated or unaccepted in the white communities in which they grew up. A nineteen-year-old college freshman, who went to mostly white schools where she was not fully accepted by white peers and was shunned by black students for attending advanced classes, explained the elation she felt when she became a member of the black college community:

It was not until I got to . . . university that I was able to say that I am black without feeling that I was somehow cutting off or ignoring the white side of me. During pre-orientation as a freshman for the first time in my life I met a huge group of people, all minorities. All like me—who had been in advanced classes. People with similar experience. Oh, it was the greatest feeling! I am not alone. It was just a week, but I think I grew up a lot. Most of my friends here are black or minorities. I have a lot more in common with them. They have helped me to see the importance of being black and it's not something to be ashamed of. One black professor especially had a great effect on the way I think now. My mom knows that I have started to consider myself as a black woman and she understands.

Feeling accepted and being given a racial home often helped these participants to reexamine the question of their racial group membership and make peace with who they were. For others—especially those with interracial or in some instances white identities—the outreach efforts and demands for assimilation by the black college community were resented. A first-year college student remembered:

Coming to college was one of the most important experiences in terms of my racial identity. All of a sudden I was faced with, You are black; you will join this organization. I started to get all the literature of the black alliances and all of a sudden it became a big issue, like What are you? Who are you going to hang with? Although it's okay to have a few white friends there is [are] limits to what is okay. I was really angry when I came here. I was like, Who the hell are you to judge me? That is why I am really excited about the biracial group.

There was also pressure to choose between black and white culture. A twenty-one-year-old college student explained:

The college situation was very confusing to me. My black friends demanded that I act black and my white friends wanted me to act white. I didn't know how to act anymore. For no matter what I did, the other side would think less of me. Blacks hated for me to listen to white music. Whites hated for me to listen to black music. I felt constantly tested by whites and constantly tested by blacks. The problem was I couldn't be me anymore. If I chose the white side I could not express the black side of me, and if I chose the black side I couldn't express the white part of me. This really got to me.

Defiance of black community expectations invited ridicule, hostile confrontations, and rejections from the black community. Because many participants did not want to pay that price, they conformed to what was expected of them. Others went into the closet with interracial self-perceptions or began compartmentalizing between a public black and private interracial or, in some instances, white identities. Finally, some simply avoided associations with the black community. For one young woman, Claudette (see chapter 1), the pressures became so intense that she left the university.

Ultimately, the exposure to the formal and informal college community invited a revisiting and rethinking of the racial identity question. Going through this process, participants often changed, modified, or reaffirmed racial self-perceptions. After such an identity transformation, participants tended to feel more firmly grounded about who they were. Their turmoil and self-doubt seemed to subside and emotional energies were freed up for learning and playing. After leaving college, as the pressures to become black became less intense, some moved once again toward a middle ground. However, the lesson that society viewed them as black had been learned more thoroughly, and therefore interracial or white identities remained frequently in the closet.

EXPOSURE TO CULTURE

The lack of black cultural exposure prevalent in many American schools was also a reality for a significant number of the men and women

Table 16

Exposure to Black and White Culture

within Pre-School and Grade School

(n = 119)

Type	Black Culture (Famous People, Books, Music, etc.)				
Time Periods	Almost Never	Some-times	Often	Almost All the Time	Not Sure or NA
Pre-School	44.5%	16.8%	5.9%	6.7%	26.1%
Grade School	33.6	44.5	10.9	6.7	4.2
Type	White Culture (Famous People, Books, Music, etc.)				
Time Periods	Almost Never	Some-times	Often	Almost all the Time	Not Sure or NA
Pre-School	7.6%	8.4%	16.0%	49.7%	19.3%
Grade School	1.7	10.1	23.5	63.0	1.7

Rows add up to 100% (except where due to rounding error.)

of this study. This gap deprived them of familiarity with their black roots and complicated their journey towards blackness. As Tables 16 and 17 demonstrate, the picture looks especially bleak for the preschool, grade-school, and high-school students. In college, however, either because of the greater availability of black history, political awareness, or the wish for greater familiarity with the black side of their racial heritage, participants seemed to make a conscious effort to fill the gap.

With exposure to black culture being the strongest predictor of low conflict about racial identity, the crucial role of in-depth knowledge of the black experience for interracial children is once more highlighted. Participants who were deprived of such awareness often associated blackness with intellectual and moral inferiority and therefore had difficulties in owning their blackness. Consistent exposure to black culture defused the disparaging societal messages regarding blacks and ultimately encouraged racial identity consolidation.

WORKING

The racial group membership question often became less important as participants were faced with the professional and personal challenges of adulthood. However, as Hawkins (1997) noted, every time people have to deny who they are, they suffer some pain. Their life force is turned

Table 17

Exposure to Black and White Culture

within High School and College

(n = 119)

Type	Black Political, Economic and Cultural Issues				
Time Periods	**Almost Never**	**Some-times**	**Often**	**Almost All the Time**	**Not Sure or NA**
High School	39.5%	37.0%	16.0%	7.6%	---
College	7.6	30.3	35.3	9.2	17.6
Type	White Political, Economic and Cultural Issues				
Time Periods	**Almost Never**	**Some-times**	**Often**	**Almost all the Time**	**Not Sure or NA**
High School	.8%	9.2%	21.8%	68.1%	---
College	2.5	7.6	37.0	35.3	17.6

Rows add up to 100% (except where due to rounding error).

inward and suppressed. They may feel ashamed, subdued, despondent, or a little deflated. The effect of these feelings may be almost unnoticeable, but as time goes on, the impact is cumulative. Aside from these ongoing emotional irritants, participants remained vulnerable to identity conflicts even after they had entered the working world. These conflicts could intensify when their identities came under fire or when they felt pressured to choose social, cultural, or political sides.

The pressure to choose between black and white friends was also present at the workplace. Too frequent association with whites invited a reputation of wanting to be white, or betraying blacks. For fair-skinned participants who opted to cross racial lines, closeness to blacks could jeopardize their intention to pass.

White-looking respondents seemed to have a special cross to bear. To avoid discrimination, some failed to mention their black roots when pursuing job opportunities. This omission frequently plagued them once they settled into a job situation. Anxiety about the deception and if and when to come out of the closet, as well as the cost involved in such a step, absorbed considerable emotional energy. The anxiety usually intensified when they witnessed racism against blacks. The fear that their confrontation of discriminatory acts against coworkers would arouse questions as to their own whiteness was often all consuming, while failure to address the wrong elicited guilt and shame.

Thus there were numerous emotional challenges that participants had to negotiate in the workplace. While they seemed to learn new and better coping skills as time went on, the upset over a world that could not let them be both black and white and to be friends with both races never seemed to quite disappear.

CHAPTER 8

Love and Color

SOCIAL EMBEDDEDNESS

The recent news that President Thomas Jefferson, one of the founding fathers of the United States, was also the father of Sally Heming's youngest son, Eston, created a tremendous stir among scholars. DNA results all but conclusively proved that the former president had a child with a woman who was his slave and interracial half sister of his deceased wife. Persistent rumors to that effect had been generally dismissed as a defamatory legend and moral impossibility by historians and by his white descendants. Jefferson had never publicly admitted to his involvement with Sally Hemings, nor did he acknowledge that they had a son together. Perhaps he sensed that such an admission might have constituted social suicide or cost him the presidency.

In general, the 1967 legal acceptance of interracial unions has not necessarily been reflected in the public arena. Attitudes against cross-racial love tend to occur on a continuum. The reasons for opposing or endorsing interracial relationships are often simplistic. On one end of the spectrum are people who completely disapprove because "racial mixing is not natural" or because "God has not intended it that way." This view fails to validate that race mixing, despite prohibitions, has occurred throughout human history. At the other end of the continuum are those who justify romance across racial lines by pronouncements like "love is colorblind." They ignore the long history of racial and sexual stereotyping and act as though, for some magical reason, racism will not enter romance (Coates, 1997). The racial identity confusion of the interracial child is often cited as a reason why interracial couples should not marry. There also has been concern (Martelle, 1970) that the increase of interracial marriage would resurrect historical concerns that racial mixing weakens the race, brings forth hostilities between whites and blacks, and could undermine the few gains made toward better understanding.

Traditionally few blacks have supported miscegenation laws. Almost three times as many more blacks than whites were in favor of mixed marriages in 1968 (Thernstrom and Thernstrom, 1997). Ironically, blacks have taken up where whites have left off. Spike Lee's 1991 film *Jungle Fever* captured the growing opposition to mixed marriages in the black community. His negative portrait of interracial love raised doubts as to whether honest relationships between blacks and whites are possible. The most vocal opponent to mixed-race marriages is Louis Farrakhan. His opposition to interracial unions is one of his main issues. A March 1996 survey showed that 52 percent of blacks approved of him, while only 30 percent opposed his views (Yankelovich Partners, 1996).

The opposition to love between blacks and whites seems especially strong among black women. Suffering from a shortage of eligible dating and marital partners, they often feel enormous resentment toward white women who "take away" their men. Deborah Rouse wrote about the deep-seated resentment that many black women feel about their men going astray with white women.

However closed-minded and racist it sounds, I don't like it. I never have. And although I'm all for hearing other folks' views, my mind is not waiting to be changed. I have participated in various "sister" groups, where black women voice their impassioned opinions about interracial relationships. Most of us have issues with brothers who favor white women: "What, we aren't good enough?" or "He's made it in life, so now he's gotta have a white woman on his arm as his trophy," we say. The smugness and disregard provide the thinnest of masks for our rage. Why be tolerant? White women already have too many things we don't: Privilege, favoritism in the workplace, and too many of our men." (p. 34)

In 1996, a controversy erupted at Brown University in Rhode Island, a bastion of progressive ideas, diversity, and sensitivity. A "Wall of

Shame" had been created (with an erasable marker) on the door of a dormitory room, bearing the names of several celebrities and Brown students involved in interracial relationships. The "Wall of Shame" was not the work of white racist but of several black women angry about what they viewed as black men's preference for white women. Thirty-one percent of the black college women interviewed by Willie and Levy (1972) held that "black students should date only other black students." Thirteen percent of the black men, 10 percent of the white men, and only 2 percent of the white women shared this attitude. Similarly, Petrioni (1971), who studied teenage interracial dating, wrote, "The fact that black students with prestige took up with white girls was a source of tension between black and white girls. More than her male counterparts, the black girl preached black separation" (p. 56).

Overall, however, the traditional taboo against interracial dating and sexual liaisons has become less stringent. Sebald (1968) proposed several factors that contributed to the breakdown of racial barriers in the pursuit of love, sex, and marriage. Among them are: (1) the legal sanctioning of interracial marriages in 1967, which prevented states from enforcing their miscegenation laws; (2) the challenge to traditional values during the youth revolt—among them, the taboos against cross-racial love; (3) the increase of blacks entering the same schools, colleges, and employment opportunities as whites, which leads to an increase of contact and opportunities to form friendships and romantic ties; and (4) the diminishing control of parents and relatives. The motto, "Do your own thing," is prevalent among the young, and families have learned to tolerate the actions of their children even if they clash with their own or socially endorsed values.

Sebald also found that black parents may be more receptive to interracial dating and marriage than white parents. Two thirds (66 percent) of the black men he interviewed believed that the race of their date would not matter to their parents, while only 30 percent of the white men felt that their parents would not mind. Barnett (1963) believed that parents who opposed their daughter's or son's interracial relationship generally did so because they feared that their children would suffer discrimination.

Despite the opposition, love between blacks and whites has become increasingly a social reality. A 1997 Gallup/USA Today poll found that of the 602 teenagers surveyed, 57 percent had dated interracially. This figure represents an increase of 17 percent from 1980.

ASSUMPTIONS ABOUT THE DYNAMICS OF CROSS-RACIAL ATTRACTION

The hypothesis that interracial couples may fall in love for the same mixture of healthy and neurotic reasons as the rest of the world is largely missing in the existing body of literature. Past and present theories about the dynamics of interracial relationships are usually negative and focus on pathology.

Powerful sexual urges have often been considered to be the reasons for such unions (Little, 1942; Murstein, 1973; Petrioni and Hirsch, 1970; Staples, 1968). White men believed that the sexual needs of a black woman were insatiable. This was a self-serving myth, which had been undoubtedly created by southern white men in the antebellum and post-bellum days. If the black woman was sexually that hungry, the white man only served as a stud to satisfy her needs, and he did not have to feel guilty about sexually exploiting her. Also, black women were sought after by white men because they were supposedly sexually free and unrepressed. In the South, black women were referred to as "wench." While this word in Elizabethan times was an innocent term, in America, it was an epithet and connoted a woman with loose morals.

The black man was supposedly uninhibited, in touch with nature's rhythm and comfortable with acting out every lewd thought the white man ever had. White men also felt convinced that the black man's sexual endowment was superior, that their penises were larger than their own. Someone actually measured the penises of African black men to prove that point. He found a mean of 4.6244 inches, which was about the same length that another researcher found in European men (Murstein, 1973). The mystique of the black male becomes even more prominent when he is an athlete. Sebald (1968) found that interracial dating among the college sample he studied indeed "gravitated towards physical and sexual preoccupation." He attributed the success of black men in dating white women to their exceptional athletic abilities and physical attractiveness.

A forbidden-fruit syndrome was thought to underlie cross-racial love (Hernton, 1965). According to this premise blacks and whites have anxiety about sex. However, because sex between two different race partners is taboo, the anxiety is much greater. Black aggressiveness and white curiosity supposedly become the driving psychological forces in the interaction between a black man and a white woman.

Davis (1941) and Merton (1941) asserted that the principle underlying black/white interracial marriage is a desire to "climb the social ladder."

An exchange is in operation whereby the black male offers his higher socioeconomic status for the preferred color-caste of a lower-class female. When Golden (1954), Heer (1974), and Monahan (1976), examined these assumptions empirically, they found no distinguishable evidence of "marrying up or marrying down" between the interracial couples they studied. Moreover, the belief that only those on the bottom of the social hierarchy would enter interracial relationships (Carlier, 1867; Calhoun, 1917; Reuter, 1918; Shannon, 1930) was dispelled by Washington (1970), Heer (1974), and Monahan (1976) when they looked empirically at these assertions. Their formal studies highlighted that cross-racial unions occurred on every socioeconomic and educational level.

Murstein (1973) has proposed rebellion against parents as a motivating force behind cross-racial liaisons. The involvement with a different race partner represents a rejection of parental authority. Also, guilt was thought to be a reason for different race mate choice (Little, 1942). Because of the abuses whites have committed against blacks, they may feel guilty for having been spared similar fates. In turn, the black man may act out a revenge motive in sleeping with a white woman to humiliate white men. Finally, deep-seated emotional disturbances such as self-destructive, exhibitionistic, sadistic, and masochistic tendencies have been attributed to those involved in cross-racial love, romance, or sexual liaisons (Little, 1942). The interracial relationship supposedly offers an opportunity to work out these personal problems.

Most of these writers have focused on the racial difference of the couple and use the willingness to ignore racial boundaries as the basis from which to explain pathological personal and interpersonal dynamics. However, to isolate the one variable and ignore a multitude of other reasons that may have motivated two people to get together is simplistic, misleading, and racist. With the narrowing of social, economic, and educational gaps, and with more integrated work and living arrangements, interracial couples may feel attracted to each other for reasons similar to those of racially homogeneous couples. As Cany Mills (1998), the editor of *Interrace Magazine*, wrote, "There is no one profile which describes people who cross intercultural/interracial boundaries. Obviously, not every human being is willing to veer from the norm." Crohn (1995) suggests that mixed-race marriages are neither signs of emotional maladjustment nor solutions to the ills of the world. He saw the increase of mixed marriages as a natural phenomenon in a world where people of different racial, cultural, and religious backgrounds live in ever greater proximity to each other. Meeting each other as friends, neighbors, or colleagues diminishes the sense of "otherness" of someone from a different background and thus reduces stranger anxiety. As a result, two people may feel attracted to each other and marry for their own special reasons, hopes, desires, dreams, needs, problems, and possibilities. Some mixed-race couples will view the culture of their partner as enriching, others as a challenge and complexity that has been added to their relationship and to their lives.

The black male/white female pair, evident in marital combinations, predominates the dating scene as well (see table 1, chapter 2). Willie and Levy (1972), who conducted a survey of four upstate New York colleges, found that 64 percent of the black men and only 36 percent of the white men reported interracial dating. Similarly, Sebald (1968), who studied Arizona State University students, found that seventy-two out of the eighty black male students he interviewed had dated interracially, while only seventeen out of one hundred and forty white male counterparts reported such experiences. Thus, black men were considerably more active in interracial love than white men. Hernton (1965) and Staples (1968) believed that the predominance of the black husband/white wife combination is a symptom of an overall racist syndrome in which the attraction between black man and white woman is based on the stereotypical notion of the black man as a symbol of sexual lust, virility, and primitive sex urges. The white woman in turn is supposedly sacred and the epitome of beauty against which all other women are measured.

Racially mixed people may be even more inclined than uniracial black or white people to disregard the color line. Not only are they a product of an interracial union and therefore biologically and emotionally directly linked to both black and white racial groups, but they may identify with their parents in choosing a racially different partner. However, due to the almost total lack of research, very little is known about their dating experiences. The 119 men and women of this study offered invaluable insight into their world of dating.

INTERRACIAL PEOPLE IN THE PURSUIT OF LOVE

Theoretically, a black/white racially mixed person crosses the color line whether they date someone white, black, or other racial background. For the purpose of the present discussion, the conventional understanding of interracial dating will be used, which is a romantic and/or sexual relationship between a socially defined white person and a socially defined person of color.

Table 18

Number of Participants Dating Partners

from Various Backgrounds in Past and Present

Participant's Dating Patterns	Mostly Black Partners	Mostly White Partners	Mostly Variety of Partners
Time Period			
Past (n = 113)	18.6%	44.2%	37.2%
Present (n = 105)	27.6	41.9%	30.5

Rows add to 100% (except where due to rounding error.)

Cross-racial dating was quite prevalent among participants (refer to Table 18). Aside from their genetically forged tie to both races and parental role model, the high number of students who participated in this study most likely also played an important role in these findings. Many of them attended universities away from home where mixed-race romance raised fewer eyebrows than in communities where they or their dating partners were known.

With the transition of time, however, the dating pattern underwent modification. The black dating partner choice became increasingly popular. This increase was statistically significant. The difficulties they encountered when dating whites and the significantly greater acceptance by blacks seemed to be important underlying reasons for this shift. For most of the men and women of this study, dating was an intensely emotional topic. Turmoil usually arose from rejections based on race, negative stereotyping, and societal opposition to cross-racial dating. Their emotional well-being as well as their racial self-perceptions were influenced by these experiences.

White Partners

The price of dating or marrying cross racially continues to be especially high for whites. Various forms of social disapproval—rejections by family and friends, job loss, disinheritance, social isolation, etc.—are frequently the cost of ignoring the color line. While some whites are willing to pay that cost, many are not. They either refrain from jumping the color line, date surreptitiously, or avoid the emotional closeness that may lead to a committed relationship. This reality is often painful and offensive to interracial people. A handsome young professional man spoke poignantly about his encounters with white women:

I felt relegated to being a sex object—there to provide them with a novel experience. It seemed as though I had no ability to offer any emotional or intellectual substance. I was merely there to perform—to offer a sex organ, so that my partner could have the desired experience. I could not enjoy myself in that way, not even from a sexual point of view, because I felt too insulted and rejected on a most fundamental human level.

Monique, a student with olive skin and long dark brown hair that reached to her waist, reported, "A lot of white guys like the idea of going out with a black girl, because they hear that they are good in bed. They are like, 'You are so exotic looking.' They like you. You are very nice and interesting, but they could never be in love with you. It's very painful."

Lack of physical evidence that they were part black seemed to decrease the chances of being rejected by whites, but if a committed relationship developed, the fear that difficulties were just around the corner were ever present. One young woman with striking blue eyes and black wavy hair kept reminding her white fiancé that they could have problems. His lack of expressed concern about her black roots created anxiety that one day his denial would backfire and he would resent her for problems they might encounter or even leave her.

Some fair-skinned participants refrained from revealing their interracial heritage until they had established a relationship. However, the questions of if and when to come out of the closet often provoked considerable turmoil. Conscious or unconscious racist attitudes and rejections often confronted them when they did. One participant who felt pressured to reveal her black roots because of having the sickle cell trait was shown a picture by her boyfriend of his crippled father. She recalled, "I know he didn't mean it like that at all. But it was like he had a secret and I had a secret. It made me think that he equated my being interracial and his father's handicap and I realized, wait a minute, something is wrong here." His response led to the breakup of their relationship. Another white-looking young woman recalled being dropped like a "hot potato" when she took her date to meet her parents. She never dated another white man after that experience.

Protecting themselves from the notion of black inferiority kept some participants from dating whites. One young man explained, "If a black man dates a white woman, it is considered a catch for the black man, because he is moving up and she is moving down in social class. I don't like that. I don't think of myself as second class, and would not like a white person to think they are dating down when they are with me."

The opposition of the dating partner's family was another obstacle when pursuing romance across racial boundaries. Parental pressures often led to breakups that could be devastating to those involved. A twenty-year-old light-brown-skinned orderly, whose white girlfriend's parents had repeatedly tried to stop their relationship, recalled:

Her parents were giving us such a hard time and we were still trying to stay together, but it was really rough. I had wished and thought about becoming Hispanic, learn the language and trying to make my hair longer and wavier. I had to ask God to please make me white so I could stay with my girlfriend. I was looking in the mirror every night, wishing I could make my skin lighter and change my eyes. I used to fantasize to have the kind of power, where her parents would see me as white, but she would see me as me. But it never came true and she finally gave up.

The grandparents of another woman's boyfriend threatened to disinherit him unless he broke up with her. She was devastated when he left her as a result of these pressures and wondered if she would ever fall in love again.

Finally, some participants refrained from dating whites because of negative repercussions from the black community. Such cross-racial dating often elicited accusations that they were not really black, a sellout, a wanna-be, or an oreo. It jeopardized their already precarious social standing. The penalties for jumping the color line were less stringent for male than for female participants. Kevin, a twenty-year-old student with the looks and identity of a black person, explained:

Being a black man, you know the motivations a white man may have when asking a black woman out. He probably may think she is exotic, a challenge, and you know that he probably uses her. Especially if the woman is attractive, there is a groundswell of anger and a general feeling among black men that this is not a good thing she is doing. She usually is labeled as a girl who likes white guys and she will be avoided by black men. I see these things and don't quite understand them, but I see myself participating in it.

One young woman commented:

A lot of my friends would go out with white guys. But they were worried about what other people think, or being ostracized by the black community. I remember one girl who dated a white person. She would tell me, "Don't tell anybody, otherwise all the black guys will be mean to me." I know that is true because they have done it. The guys think it's different when they go out with a white girl. They say, "We are just using them. They don't really mean anything. We have more respect for black females."

Participants who consistently dated whites were found to have white identities as well as significant degrees of conflict about racial group membership. Whether they pursued romance with whites because they identified with them, or whether they felt pressured to negate their blackness in order to be accepted into the family or social circle of a white partner is not quite clear from the findings of this study. A significant and negative relationship between acceptance of white dating partners and the diminished black identity points to the validity of the latter scenario.

Participants who spent their teenage years in white communities had little chance of finding suitable partners. While some participants seemed to cope and sublimate with other interests, others became withdrawn and questioned their self-worth. One very attractive and bright young woman, who grew up in a white suburb, related that she felt "socially stunted" by that experience. Participants felt usually "amazed" by the number of people interested in them once they entered college or a racially diverse workplace. Thus leaving the white communities in which they grew up frequently offered an important opportunity to heal some of the scars of feeling unwanted.

Black Partners

Dating blacks seemed much easier. The societal blessing of such a union, sharing a common culture and experience as people of color as well as greater acceptance by the dating partner and their families made black romance increasingly attractive. As one young professional man explained, "Blacks are not as racist as whites. With whites it is always an issue whether you are going to be accepted by their families and friends. If you date a black person you don't have to worry about that." Being in an environment where their blackness was not an issue was most comforting and freeing to the men and women of this study.

Respondents whose physical characteristics clearly showed evidence of black roots at times enjoyed greater popularity than those who looked white. For a black person to date someone whose racial features resembled the white oppressor could evoke anger and contempt—especially from militant blacks. Consequently, some blacks avoided romantic ties with Caucasian-looking participants altogether or did not allow themselves to get too close. This left a bitter taste in some respondents. Monique explained:

Black men think you are attractive. They like you, but they could never take you home to their parents, because of looking white. It's very strange. It's here in this college community where people try to be more politically powerful. If you are sort of deviating from the race then you are undermining the whole thing. It's a blacker than thou thing. I am being very skeptical now. I try to get to know people very well before I get involved.

Some of the parents also seemed to be more welcoming to darker-skinned participants. As one fair-skinned and blue-eyed interracial male high-school senior explained:

With the white parents, it's sort of a traditional prejudice, but with blacks—and that is true for friendships too—it is really a paranoia, an unrest about it more than a dislike. It's almost like they are afraid of what is going to happen to their daughter. It is not so much that they would not like them to see me. They may try to make a point to her that white people can't be trusted.

Some of the white-looking men and women tried to compensate for their own lack of physical blackness by dating someone much darker than they were. With their white physical appearance failing to reflect their psychic makeup and their identification with the black world, the black dating partner choice brought the emotional and physical discrepancy into greater harmony. At the same time it legitimized their black racial group membership to the outside world. A twenty-one-year-old student with white skin and long blond curly hair explained, "People go by what they see. Being with a black man reinforces that I am black too. My children would not understand the black side of me, if I married a white man. If I marry a black man it will be there."

Over half (56.3 percent) of the people in this study reported that their racial identities were affected by the dating experience. Participants who consistently dated blacks had significantly strengthened black identities and enjoyed significant conflict reduction. Again, it is possible that they had existing black identities and therefore felt more attracted to blacks than whites. It is also possible that their black identifications were reinforced by the intimate connection with a black person. A medium-brown-skinned college senior elaborated, "When a white person doesn't want to date you, you realize that they are prejudiced against you because you are black, not because you are mixed. This leads me to believe that I am only perceived as black and in turn I perceive myself as black." A twenty-one-year-old student with a white identity until his teenage years explained, "I know there are so many people who see a white and black together and say, 'Uck, ick we can't have that!' Society says blacks will marry blacks and whites will marry whites. The dating experience made me realize if you are interracial it's much easier to go into a black than a white world."

Overall, pursuing love and marriage in the black world was less stressful and presented fewer social and emotional stumbling blocks for participants. Whether the ability to define oneself by one or more than one race will affect whom interracial people date and marry remains to be seen.

CHAPTER 9

Being Well

RESILIENCE

Writers, moviemakers, and social scientists at the beginning of this century created a portrait of interracial people as "lost souls" whose inner turmoil left them psychologically and emotionally maladjusted. This picture was confirmed in the late 1960s when health professionals began to study a few interracial families and their children in mental health clinics and generalized from the findings to the overall population of mixed-race families.

The men and women who participated in this nonclinical study suggest that the image of the "tragic mulatto" is valid for some mixed race people, but not for other. Rather, adjustment for them occurred on a continuum and was influenced by experiences within their immediate and extended social milieu as well as physical, personal, and demographic factors. While many experienced emotional turmoil about their racial identities, these conflicts did not necessarily prevent them from enjoying positive lives. Many were high achievers and were found in prestigious universities. They had good or average jobs and stable relationships, were socially adept in both the black and white circles, and were able to enjoy life. It seems that the difficulties they encountered growing up as mixed-race persons in a racist social climate made many of them resilient. Stepakoff and Bowleg (1997) postulate that the marginal social status of interracial children may serve as an "inoculation" against other traumatic social experiences. Some participants, either because of growing up a dysfunctional family, excessive stress in their social milieu, or their own constitutional weakness were unable to adapt. The emotional turmoil and confusion they experienced about racial group membership and the racism they had encountered rendered them socially and emotionally handicapped. They seemed socially isolated, filled with despair and hopelessness, and were dysfunctional in various areas of their lives.

The attitudes toward being interracial differed among the participants. While some felt strengthened and enriched by their dual racial heritage, others felt burdened. A twenty-two-year-old woman said:

I look at it as a positive thing being interracial. It's good—I got to see both sides of the coin and I get to experience a lot of things that my friends have not experienced. I think it has made me a much more intelligent person, not bookwise, but intelligent as far as life and what is important. I think it made me a stronger person, because I had to sit and work things out in my head. Being mixed made me kind of philosophical in my thinking. It definitely made me a better and stronger person.

A young chaplain explained, "Certainly the racism in my community had a profound effect on the way I see myself. It caused a lot of confusion. The most positive side of it, however, was a real longing to understand what that meant and to find a home in terms of both sides of myself. As often as I was distraught over the confusion, the real gift is to understand both sides. It certainly helps in my work." Others felt less positive. A twenty-five-year-old woman with a strong interracial identity explained at the end of the interview, "I think there were certain periods of my life where it seemed like life would be so much easier if I were just white or if I were just black—depending on which period it was— and especially the way this country is. It's a 'huger' burden in some respects to be interracial than to be black—yes and no—but anyway, it is a different burden." Perhaps the freedom to be *both* black and white rather than to be black *or* white will lift some of this burden for mixed-race people. For the rest of this country, a less rigid way of thinking about race will not only be necessary as the racial boundaries between groups continue to become blurred, but it will be a healthier way to look at the world.

PROVIDING A HEALTHY FAMILY ENVIRONMENT

Interracial children need the love, care, protection, support, and honesty that all children need. However, because of their ambiguous racial status and their vulnerability to discrimination, the interracial child has some special needs. To meet those and to enhance psychosocial adjustment, parents need to communicate openly about racial issues. While validating the biracial heritage of their children, parents should prepare them that the outside world may view them as black. If the phenotype of the child is Caucasian, the difference between physical and societal messages should be addressed. For society might view the child as white, but when it becomes known that he or she has a black parent, that child most likely will be regarded as black, even though the new system of racial classification will offer other choices. It is unlikely that the American public will change its mind overnight about the "one drop of black blood" rule. The child needs to be prepared for that reality.

Given the discrepant internal and external messages that interracial children are subjected to, they are prone to racial identity fluctuations. Parents should not become overly alarmed when they see evidence of that. Excessive pressure in either the white or black direction may cause conflict and lead to premature closure of the question, Who am I? Rather, the reality of their dual racial background should be consistently confirmed and pride in both backgrounds encouraged. Possible discrepancies between racial appearance and racial identity may need to be addressed. For instance, a light-brown interracial child or adolescent with a white identity and predilection to "pass" may need help in understanding that crossing racial lines is not an option for them. Ultimately, the child should be assured that he or she can be both black and white.

If at all possible, interracial children should be raised in a racially mixed community. The greater racial tolerance that characterizes these neighborhoods enables them to embrace both parts of their racial background. Both cultures should be represented and celebrated within the home so that they will become familiar with the practices, rituals, art forms, accomplishments, and struggles of both cultures. Such exposure promises to enrich their minds as well as their souls. It will encourage self-acceptance because it is a powerful antidote against racial prejudice. Contact with both sides of the family should be nurtured, so that they have black, white, and possibly interracial role models they can identify with and learn from. Since the United States is a white culture-dominated society, special efforts should be made to expose interracial children to the less represented black cultural heritage. These children should be taught about black history and contemporary black issues. They should learn about slavery, the Civil War, black leaders, black achievements, etc.

Interracial children must cope in a social milieu that not only may discriminate against them because of their blackness or whiteness, but also because of their biracial background. Therefore, racial prejudice should be addressed in the widest and most personal sense (Spivey, 1984). These children should learn that the family may not judge people by the color of their skin, but that many people in society do. They should become familiar with the nuances, symbolism, language and gestures of racism and learn how to protect themselves in response to hostile behavior or overfriendliness (Ladner, 1977). Teaching coping mechanisms should be done in an age-appropriate fashion. For instance, young children may need to be taught to identify racist behavior and report it to a parent or teacher who then may intervene for them, while adolescents will need to learn how to deal with racism personally.

The black parent may be more adept in preparing a child to cope with racial bigotry. Never having gone through life as a person of color, the white parent may not react to racism the way a black person does. Consequently, he or she may lack the necessary coping skills and may feel anxious or inadequate in teaching a child how to survive in a racist environment.

Finally, the tensions that separate people of different racial backgrounds should never exist inside the home. The parents must examine themselves about racial prejudice or color biases they may have internalized by living in a racist world. Such self-examination will enhance their ability to make certain that their children will not be victimized by such attitudes. The race card should not be played when conflict arises within the parent-child or the husband-wife relationship. Derogatory comments about the child's whiteness or blackness can be devastating. Similarly, racist remarks by one parent about the other parent's racial group is traumatic not only for the spouse but also for the child.

Parents who themselves may be overwhelmed by accusations of selling out, being see as deviant or morally deficient, or suffered rejection by their families and friends may be in denial about their child's struggle. Or they may try to protect their child by avoiding discussions about upsetting experiences within the family or the outside world. Such avoidance can create intense anxiety in children. A white-skinned, blue-eyed young professional man whose mother's family did not accept his mixed-race father, talked about the terrible impact the family secrecy had on him and his sister.

The family disharmony and not talking about it made it more difficult to deal with the racial issue. My parents tried to protect us by "going away" and not really explaining what was going on. The message was "Don't worry; everything will be okay," although it really wasn't. My father told me so little about himself and his past. I found out mainly from other people. For me that caused a real emotional detachment from my parents. I became very much a loner and over-achiever. My sister withdrew and developed anorexia nervosa. She is a very fragile person. I was not sure until high school which race I was.

Interracial family and student organizations have mushroomed since the early 1980s in many cities and universities (see Appendix C). They provide a much needed support system to interracial families and their children. The new racial classification regulations implemented at the turn of the new century are designed to correct some of the civil rights violations committed against interracial people. Hopefully this change will enable mixed-race parents to teach their children that they are, and culturally can be, part of both racial groups.

MENTAL HEALTH

Despite the interracial baby boom that has taken place since the miscegenation laws were abolished in 1967, theories about developmental issues of mixed-race people are lacking. Their experiences are rarely reflected in either the mass media or professional journals. Mental health professionals need to expand their thinking to include the emotional impact of negative stereotyping, discrimination, and oppression of all people of color, including interracial people. Greater understanding is also needed as to the underlying psychological forces that lead to racial bigotry and racist abuses. Such understanding helps to prevent victimization based on race, culture, or ethnicity and will make this country a better place.

Most American therapists have limited cross-cultural experience. They come from rather homogeneous backgrounds and are not fluent in any language but English. Many prefer to work with clients from their own social, economic, cultural, or religious background. Cultural forces are bypassed in favor of intrapsychic factors to explain personal differences. This cross-cultural narrowness is unfortunate, for it encourages a myopic vision of the dynamics of the patient and often leads to a "well meaning but naïve ethnocentrism" that prevents therapists from seeing their own limitations (Fish, 1996).

Psychoanalysis for the most part has emphasized the psychology of the individual, whether in drive, behavioral, or object relations theories. Similarly, traditional psychodynamic and cognitive theories do not, for the most part, account for race, poverty, and ethnicity. This is difficult to understand, given the powerful impact that these factors have on the personality structure and their prevalence throughout the world—including the United States (Javier, Herron, and Yanos, 1998).

For decades social scientists saw interracial people as emotionally maladjusted because of their mixed racial makeup. The psychological toll caused by society's rendering them invisible and the constant unfavorable images they receive of themselves and their families have been largely ignored. Racism affects interracial people in very concrete and real ways. It can hurt, humiliate, enrage, and confuse them and ultimately undermine their development or prevent them from reaching their potentials as individuals or as community members.

Institutional racism and racial bigotry from both the white and the black side of the racial divide are major stressors in the lives of many mixed-race people. Harrell (2000) observed that there are at least six types of racism connected to stress. These are "racism related to life events, vicarious racism experiences, daily racism microstressors, chronic contextual stress, collective experiences of racism and the transgenerational transmission of group trauma" (p. 45). Most mixed-race people are subjected to some or all of these stressors during the course of their lives.

This is not to deny that any given interracial person also develops feelings of inferiority or other emotional scars within their families or from other people in their immediate or extended social milieu. To what degree they do so is influenced by their personal characteristics as well as the frequency and intensity of the toxic stimuli. However, to ignore powerful environmental stimuli in favor of intrapsychic forces would certainly be a tragic clinical shortcoming. As Myers and King (1983) suggest:

The analysis of mental health in a class-caste society . . . cannot . . . be made simply on the basis of the presence or absence of illness symptoms. It must necessarily include the analysis of the transactional process between individual and social class, and the social structures . . . that create the conditions of differential mental health vulnerability as a function of social class and race. . . . The concept of mental health in an oppressive reality must also include the active commitment to personal and social transformation. (p. 297)

Without cross-cultural understanding the therapist is not only handicapped in seeing the client's experience through his or her eyes but also in asking pertinent questions. Ignorance or evasiveness are major roadblocks to getting accurate information. Diagnostic and prognostic evaluations become distorted and so does the treatment process. Ring (2000), based on the work of Wrenn (1962) and Pederson (1991), defines a culturally encapsulated therapist as someone who sees reality within a singular cultural framework, lacks sensitivity to cultural differences and assumes that his or her view is the only valid one. It is also someone who fails to have reasons or proof for their assumptions and protects these assumptions without regard for their rationality. Finally, the culturally rigid therapist is concerned about technique and interprets the behavior of others by using him- or herself as a criterion.

Fish (1996) suggests that therapists should be knowledgeable in anthropology and sociology as a supplement to psychology. He believes that a pairing of these disciplines will help therapists toward a more complete understanding of their patients. Due to the marginal social position and social mischaracterization of interracial people, these three social sciences are especially closely intertwined for them. To ignore that reality will seriously undermine the understanding of their experiences and ultimately their psychic development.

SOCIETY

Since one's psychological and social well-being are closely intertwined, one must consider them in consort. In a society where millions of people defy rigid racial categorizations, the new system of race classification, implemented by the Office of Management and Budget (OMB) and adopted by the Clinton administration in 1997, promises to make the journey toward a healthy identity for mixed people a less confusing and lonely odyssey. Being able to identify oneself as a member of more than one race will enable interracial people to accurately define their dual racial background and thus encourage a sense of wholeness and well-being. While these are important emotional gains, the sociological benefit of such a ruling has been questioned.

Civil rights groups are fearful that diluting the number of people who are classified as black would diminish their ability to secure social and economic justice. Some minority critics contend that the drive for a change in racial classification is a means of doing away with affirmative action and government programs. They contend that by dividing into parts a person's racial mix or in the removal of members from existing groups, blacks as well as mixed race people would lose full political representation and their fair share of federally funded programs.

How people define themselves on census forms will echo through public policy. For instance, the Justice Department uses racial information from the census to determine voting patterns and evaluate redistricting proposals under the Voting Rights Act. Lawyers in employment discrimination suits will at times try to prove that a company is racially biased by comparing the number of blacks in particular jobs with the proportion of African Americans in the local population. Such litigation would be greatly affected if a significant number of socially defined blacks listed themselves as being more than one race and the government counted them something other than black. City and state planners use racial data to determine allocations to needy communities. For instance, the amount of resources that go to black communities are directly connected to the number of blacks counted in the census.

Spencer (1997) feared that the establishment of a separate "multiracial" category would have tragic consequences for this country. Similar to South Africa, Spencer argues, where mixed-race people are classified as "coloured," such a splintering of blacks and multiracial people would establish a racial hierarchy in which multiracial people assume a higher position than blacks. Consequently, a deeper racial division would be encouraged.

While some multiracialists share these concerns, the Association of Multiethnic Americans insists that mixed-race people should be counted separately. They want a multiracial category or an elimination of race altogether. When the Clinton administration introduced new rules for the 2000 census, the debate of how to utilize such data began to heat up. The suggestion of the OMB (1997) that a person checking two or even three boxes to define their racial background would still be counted solely as "black" or "African American" was met by some multiracialists with anger and defiance. They argued that this approach "is the 'politically correct' version of the old 'one drop rule' " and urged interracial people toward "civil disobedience" by checking "white," "every box on the form," "American Indian" or not returning a Census form at all (*Interracial Voice*, December 1998). Charles Byrd, who runs the *Interracial Voice*, site feels that "we need to get rid of these stupid boxes altogether."

With the expansion of America's multiracial population, the traditional system of racial categorization has become increasingly outdated. Its rigid racial categories no longer reflect the racial makeup of a growing number of the American citizens. In 1970 only 720,000 people (less than one half of 1 percent of the population) indicated some other category of the census. On the 1990 census about ten million (about 4 percent of the entire population) checked the official "other" category, which first appeared that year. Of the eight million write-ins under the "other" category, 253,000 people defined themselves as "multiracial" or "interracial" or as "black-white" or "Asian-white" and so on.

The new standards for federal data on race and ethnicity provide demographers with a much more accurate portrait of America's multiracial citizenry. For instance, the 2000 census forms offer fourteen boxes representing six races (white, black, American Indian or Alaska Native, Asian Indian, other Asian and Pacific Islander—or "some other race.") There are also subcategories. All in all there are sixty-three possible combinations of racial identity (Schemo, 2000).

How agencies and the many users of the race and ethnicity data utilize the data was initially vague. Joseph Salvo, a member of the national committee advising the Census Bureau, explained about the upcoming count: "It is being worked out as we go" (Schemo, 2000). The utilization of data depended on the "judgment of the users." Federal agencies with similar or related responsibilities were encouraged to use the same method of tabulation.

The guidelines stated: "To foster comparability across data collections carried out by various agencies, it is useful for those agencies to report responses of more than one race using some standardized tabulation or formats" (p. 5). This *laissez-faire* approach created considerable confusion.

In an effort to clarify the ruling, the office of Management and Budget issued a new directive on March 10, 2000. The new ruling stipulates that people who define themselves on this year's census as white and as a minority will be counted as a minority by government agencies who monitor discrimination and enforcing civil rights laws. Sally Katzen, counselor to the director of the OMB, said that the decision was designed to offer certain protections to those who have suffered discrimination in the past.

The new policy was hailed by civil rights groups who had expressed concern that the new system of racial classifications would reduce the number of people who are considered black, Asian or American Indian and would therefore jeopardize their civil and voting rights. However, they had concerns about the implementation of the new policy. For instance, the White House has not addressed the issue of comparing the new multiracial data with data from the past which is important for monitoring school segregation and other racial problems.

Groups of mixed-race families who resented the old racial categories that forced them to choose one race for their offspring, were disappointed with the new policy. Levonne Gaddy, a Tuscon mixed-race activist said: "It feels like no progress at all." Some intellectuals, who have been critical of affirmative action programs, acknowledge the benefits of the new policy, but also see serious drawbacks. Stephan Thernstrom, a Harvard history professor said: "I think it's a step forward to stop forcing every American into one racial box, which the Census Bureau has always done. On the other hand, in some ways it's even worse. It's not just one of four or five boxes they are putting you into, it's 63!" (Holmes, 2000). The American Anthropological Association asserted that American society must find more accurate ways of classifying its increasingly diverse population. Since many Americans consider race and ethnicity as interchangeable, they suggest "ethnic group" as a viable option.

Revamping of our system of racial classification is a complex and controversial undertaking. The fight over how to count people will continue. For the issue of how to categorize interracial people is a microcosm of the larger issue that confronts this country in this new century as the "browning of America" continues. The term "minority" has become a misnomer in America as whites of European roots are being increasingly replaced by people of color in many urban areas as well as smaller communities (Nevid and Goodman, 1998). Because the issue of race is such a vital and deeply complex one, strong leadership is needed to promote reconciliation of the various interests.

Social scientists must take extreme care not to turn the clock back on the well-being of those who have been oppressed and held back by racist practices. The freedom to define accurately the combination of one's racial background will be enormously beneficial for the psychic well-being of mixed-race individuals. At the same time, being counted as black in the census will safeguard the civil rights of mixed-race people as well as blacks. Until we can live in a more ideal world where there are no boxes, and the civil rights of all people in this country are more firmly grounded, such an approach is pragmatic despite its bedeviling qualities to both the analyst of census data and those who oppose rigid racial categorization.

Because race continues to be a potent cultural and political marker, the need to collect such data most likely will not disappear in the near future. For those who cannot find a racial category they like, they may follow the example of some of the men and women of this study. They opted for the "other" race category and added that they were members of the human race. Whether these participants were mere dissidents to social conventions, dreamers, idealists or pioneers of a gentler society remains to be seen.

Demographic Characteristics of the Study Participants and Their Parents

	Participant	Father of Participant	Mother of Participant	Parents of Participant
AGE:				
18-20	55.5%	----	----	----
21-23	26.9			
24-26	8.4			
27-29	5.0			
30-32	2.5			
33-35	1.6			
Mean: 21.4				
Standard Deviation: 3.41				
GENDER:				
Male	41.2	---	---	---
Female	58.8			
MARITAL STATUS:				
Single - never married	89.1	---	---	11.8%
Living with partner	3.4	---	---	---
Married	5.9	---	---	41.2
Separated	1.7	---	---	8.4
Divorced	---	---	---	32.8
Widowed	---	---	---	5.0
Both deceased	---	---	---	.8

	Participant	Father of Participant	Mother of Participant	Parents of Participant
EDUCATION:				
Some grade school	----	3.4%	----	----
Grade school	----	.8	.8%	----
Some high school	3.4%	1.7	4.2	----
High school graduate	14.3	22.7	16.0	----
Some college	61.3	15.1	23.0	----
College graduate	16.0	11.8	19.3	----
Some graduate school	2.5	9.2	7.6	----
Graduate school	2.5	31.1	28.6	----
NA	----	4.2	----	----
OCCUPATIONS:				
Executive/proprietor	.8	----	----	----
Manager/proprietor	1.7	----	----	----
Administrative person	.8	----	----	----
Clerical and sales	2.5	----	----	----
Skilled workers	19.3	----	----	----
Semi-skilled workers	1.7	----	----	----
Unskilled workers	.8	----	----	----
Student	72.3	----	----	----

	Participant	Father of Participant	Mother of Participant	Parents of Participant
RACE:				---
Black	---	78.2%	20.2%	
White	---	20.1	79.8	
Interracial	100%	1.7	---	

NUMBER OF SIBLINGS:

	Participant
1	27.7%
2	19.3
3	24.4
4	8.4
5	5.0
6	2.5
7	2.5
8	.8
9	---
10	---
None	9.2

Mean: 2.62

Standard
Deviation: 1.60

Pathdiagram of Multivaried Relationships of Racial Identity, Conflict, and Self-esteem

The diagram shows the most important factors that influence racial identity, conflict, and self-esteem; coefficients are betas.

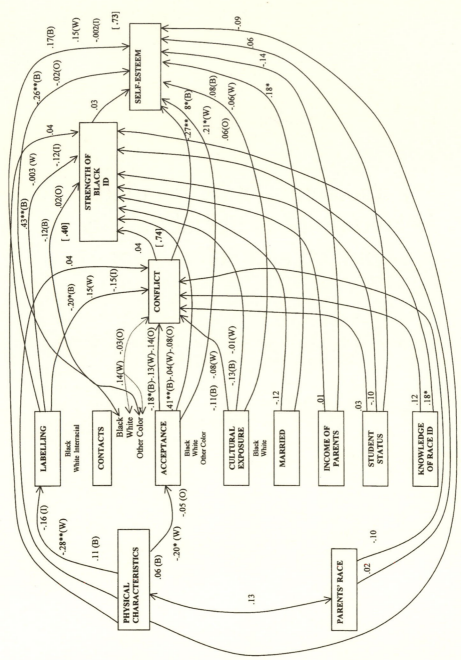

Note: n = 119; *p ≤ .05; ** p ≤ .01.

126

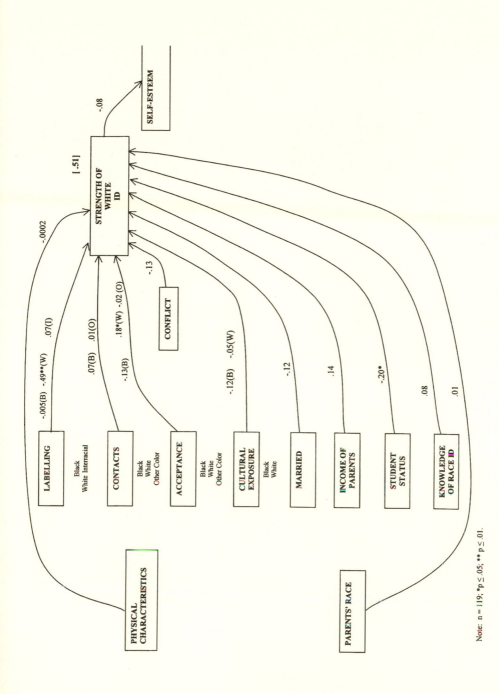

Note: n = 119; *p ≤ .05; ** p ≤ .01.

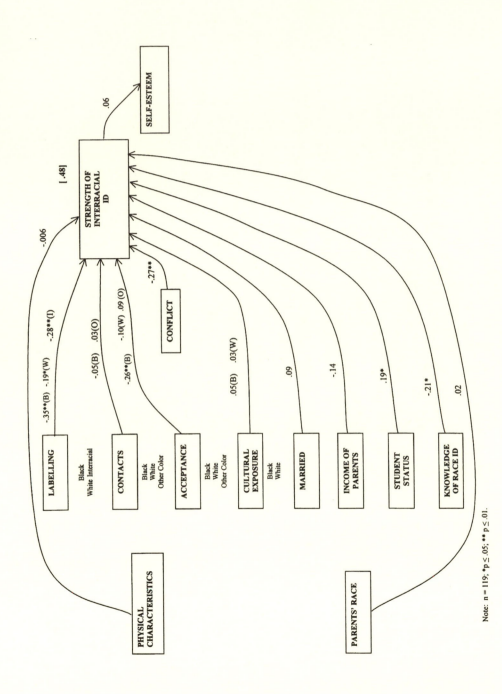

SELF-ESTEEM

.06

[.48]

STRENGTH OF
INTERRACIAL
ID

-.006

-.35**(B) -.19*(W)

-.28***(I)

LABELLING

Black
White Interracial

-.05(B) .03(O)

CONTACTS

Black
White
Other Color

-.26**(B)

-.10(W) .09 (O)

ACCEPTANCE

Black
White
Other Color

-.27**

CONFLICT

.05(B) .03(W)

CULTURAL
EXPOSURE

Black
White

.09

MARRIED

-.14

INCOME OF
PARENTS

.19*

STUDENT
STATUS

-.21*

KNOWLEDGE
OF RACE ID

.02

PHYSICAL
CHARACTERISTICS

PARENTS' RACE

Note: n = 119; *p ≤ .05; ** p ≤ .01.

128

APPENDIX C

National Interracial Support/ Advocacy Groups

ARKANSAS

A Place for Us
c/o Rita Bowens
P.O. Box 104
Little Rock, AR 72203
Phone (501) 791–0988

CALIFORNIA

A Place for Us
Box 357
Gardena, CA 90248–7857
Phone (213) 779–1717 (24-hour Message Center)
Web Profile

I-PRIDE (Interracial Intercultural Pride)
Box 11811
Berkeley, CA 94712–11811
Phone (510) 653–1929

IMAGE
Box 4382
San Diego, CA 92164
Phone (619) 527–2850

MASC (Multiracial Americans of Southern California)
12228 Venice Boulevard, #452
Los Angeles, CA 90066
Phone (310) 836–1535

Race Unity—Matters!
of Northern California
4309 Linda Vista Avenue
Napa, CA 94558

National Multi-Ethnic Families Association (NaMEFA)
2073 North Oxnard Boulevard, Suite 172
Oxnard, CA 93030
Our official journal, locally anyway, is the monthly Nuestra America
    (Spanish/English) which has a web page at http://www.latinoweb.
    com/nuestram/

Men of All Colors Together
San Francisco-Richard Brownscombe, Co-Chair

Mixed Heritage Multiracial Alliance of Carson High School
"Committed to Building Bridges Between the Races"
Organization Founder/Educator: Karen Dabney
Phone (562) 437–5669

COLORADO

F.C. (Families of Color) Communique
c/o Dr. C. Lessman
Box 478
Fort Collins, CO 80522
Phone (303) 223–9658

Center for Study of Biracial Children
c/o Francis Wardle, Ph.D.
2300 South Krameria Street
Denver, CO 80222
Phone (303) 692–9008

Humanity
c/o Martin L. Scruggs
P.O. Box 481692
Denver, CO 80248–1692
Phone (303) 832–6269

DISTRICT OF COLUMBIA

The Interracial Family Circle of Washington
Box 53291
Washington, DC 20009
Voice Mail (202) 393–7866 or (800) 500–9040
The Interracial Family Circle's Website

FLORIDA

Unity Multiracial Social Group
P.O. Box 2902
Orange Park, FL 32073–2902
Phone (904) 276–6668

BRANCH (Biracial & Natural Children)
Box 50051
Lighthouse Point, FL 33074
Phone (305) 781–6798

Interracial Couple & Family Network of Tallahassee
2001 Holmes Street
Tallahassee, FL 32310
Phone (904) 576–6734

A Place for Us
Naples, FL, Chapter
c/o Cherie Byrd
Phone (813) 732–6996

Harmony
Box 16996
West Palm Beach, FL 33416
Phone (407) 582–2182

Tallahassee Multiracial Connection
2001 Holmes Street
Tallahassee, FL 32310
Phone (904) 576–6734

GEORGIA

Interracial Family Alliance
Box 450473
Atlanta, GA 31145

Interracial Family Alliance
Box 9117
Augusta, GA 30906

Interracial Family Alliance
c/o Tonia and Glenn Thomas
Athens, GA
Phone (706) 353–0640

ILLINOIS

Biracial Family Network
Box 3214
Chicago, IL 60654
Phone (773) 288–3644

Families for Interracial Awareness
Northern Chicago area
c/o Linda Thomas
Phone (708) 869–7117

Sherry Blass
c/o Tapestry
40 Francis Avenue
Crystal Lake, IL 60014

Interracial Family Network
c/o Dickelle Fonda
Box 5380
Evanston, IL 60204–5380
Phone (708) 491–9748

Child International
4121 Crestwood
Northbrook, IL 60062

Linda Russo
c/o Adoptive Parents Together
427 North Wheaton Avenue
Wheaton, IL 60187

North Shore Race Unity Task Force
536 Sheridan Road
Wilmette, IL 60091

Dialogue Racism, Inc.
c/o Charles Young
P.O. Box 110
Evanston, IL 60204
Phone (708) 492–0123

KENTUCKY

Northern Kentucky Multiracial Alliance
Pat DiMartile
Phone (502) 331–2373

MARYLAND

Interracial Military Families
P.O. Box 1015
Upper Marlboro, MD 20773

MASSACHUSETTS

Students of Mixed Heritage
SU 3187, Williams College
Williamstown, MA 01267
Phone (413) 597–3354

New England Alliance of Multiracial Families
P.O. Box 148
West Medford, MA 02156
Phone (617) 965–3287

Multiracial Family Group of Western Massachusetts
P.O. Box 1216
Amherst, MA 01004–1216
Phone (413) 256–0502

MICHIGAN

Multiracial Group at U. of Michigan
c/o Karen E. Downing
1222 Undergraduate Library
Ann Arbor, MI 48109–1185
Phone (313) 763–5084 or (313) 764–4479

Biracial and Interracial Family & Friends (BIFF)
c/o Dr. Zawdie K. Abiade
Burton Heights U.M.C.
100 Burton Street, S.E.
Grand Rapids, MI 49507

Society for Interracial Families
Box 4942
Troy, MI 48099

MISSOURI

Multiracial Family Circle of Kansas City
P.O. Box 32414
Kansas City, MO 64171
Contact: Kevin—Phone (816) 353–8689
E-mail: MFCircle@aol.com (Kevin L. Barber)

NEW JERSEY

Multiracial Family Support Group
c/o Bobbi Joels
265 Hempstead Drive
Somerset, NJ 08873
Phone (732) 296–0734

G.I.F.T. (Getting Interracial/cultural Families Together)
P.O. Box 1281
Montclair, NJ 07042
c/o Irene Rottenberg
Phone (973) 783–0083

E-mail: NJGIFT@aol.com
Web profile: members.aol.com/NJGIFT/index.html

G.I.F.T. (Getting Interracial/cultural Families Together)
P.O. Box 811
Lakewood, NJ 08701
c/o Betty Turko
Phone (908) 364–8136
Fax: (908) 367–2755

InterRacial Life
c/o Dave Seibel
2 George Street
East Brunswick, NJ 08816
Phone (908) 390–7316

4C (Cross Cultural Couples & Children) of Plainsboro, NJ
P.O. Box 8
Plainsboro, NJ 08536–4104
c/o Lisa Edwards
Phone (609) 275–9352 (eves)

NEW YORK

BIRONY (Bi-Racials of New York)
Phone (212) 979–0967

Interracial Identity
c/o Noel A. Trowers
228–26 Edgewood Avenue
Rosedale, NY 11413
Phone (718) 978–6524

A Place for Us
c/o Valerie Wilkins-Godbee
P.O. Box 859
Peekskill, NY 10566
Phone (914) 736–0536

Creole-American Genealogical Society, Inc.
c/o Ms. P. Fontaine, Director
Box 3215, Church Street Station
New York, NY 10008

Interracial Club of Buffalo
Box 400 (Amherst Branch)
Buffalo, NY 14226
Phone (716) 875–6958

Multiethnic Women for Medial Fairness
P.O. Box 859
Peekskill, NY 10566

Interracial Ministries of America
5805 Aqua Court
Charlotte, NC 28215

LIFE
Box 14123
Raleigh, NC 27620

T.I.M.E. (Triangle Interracial and Multicultural Experience)
c/o Marsha Alston
15A Woodbridge Drive
Chapel Hill, NC 27516

OHIO

Cincinnati Multiracial Alliance
Box 17163
St. Bernard, OH 45217
Phone (513) 791–6023

SWIRLS Ministry
Bob & Gerry Schneider
132 East South Street
Fostoria, OH 44830
Phone (419) 435–0325

Heights Multicultural Group
c/o Sylvia Billups
South Euclid, OH 44121
Phone (216) 382–7912

Rainbow Families of Toledo (adoption support group)
c/o Nancy Shanks
1920 South Shore Boulevard
Oregon, OH 43618
Phone (419) 693–9259

OREGON

Honor Our New Ethnic Youth (HONEY)
454 Willamette Avenue, #213
Eugene, OR 97401
Phone (503) 342–3908

Interracial Family Network
Box 12505
Portland, OR 97212

PENNSYLVANIA

Multiracial Americans of Philadelphia
c/o Joycelyn Damita
Box 58722
Philadelphia, PA 19102–8722
Phone (215) 492–8761, ext. 2

Rainbow Circle
Broadfield Assoc.
Box 242
Chester, PA 19016

SOME Families
1798 Unionville-Lenape Road
West Chester, PA 19382
Phone (215) 793–1533

One Race
P.O. Box 58722
Philadelphia, PA 19102–8722

TEXAS

The Interracial Family and Social Alliance of Dallas-Ft. Worth
Box 35109
Dallas, TX 75235–0109
Phone (214) 559–6929

A Place For Us
Dallas, TX Chapter
c/o Brad & Amy Russell
Phone (214) 517–1498

Interracial Family Alliance
Box 16248
Houston, TX 77222–6248

Center for the Healing of Racism
Box 27327
Houston, TX 77227
Phone (713) 526–7223 (526-RACE)

VERMONT

International Institute for the Healing of Racism
Route 113, Box 232
Thetford, VT 05074
Phone (802) 785–2627

WASHINGTON

Interracial Network
Box 344
Auburn, WA 98071–0344

References

Adaire, F. 1984. "Coopersmith Self-Esteem Inventories." In *Test Critiques*, Vol. 1, edited by D. Keyser, and R. C. Sweetland. Kansas City: Test Corporation of America.

Adams, P. 1973. "Counseling with Interracial Couples and Their Children in the South." In *Interracial Marriage: Expectations and Realities*, edited by I. Stuart and L. E. Abt. New York: Grossman.

Arnold, M. C. 1984. "The Effect of Racial Identification on Self-Concept in Interracial Children." Ph.D. diss., St. Louis University.

Baldwin, J. 1963. "A Talk to Teachers." *Saturday Review*: 42–43.

———. 1985. *The Evidence of Things Not Seen*. New York: St. Martin's/Marek.

Banks, C. M. 1985. "The Effect of the Mother's Self-Esteem and of Social Environmental Support on the Acceptance of the Handicapped Child." Ph.D. Diss., New York University.

Baptiste, P., Jr. 1985. "The Contemporary Interracial Child." *Communique: Interracial Family Alliance*, April. Houston, Texas: 1, 7.

Barnett, L. 1963. "Student's Anticipations of Persons and Arguments Opposing Interracial Dating." *Marriage and Family Living*, August.

Barr, S., and M. Fletcher. 1997. "U.S. Proposes Multiple Racial Identification for 2000 Census." *The Washington Post*, 9 July, p. A1.

Barzun, J. 1965. *Race: A Study in Superstition*. New York: Harper and Row.

Berzon, J. R. 1974. "Neither Black nor White: The Mulatto Character in American Fiction." Ph.D. diss., New York University. Dissertation Abstracts International 1975, 35, 10-A, 6707. University Microfilms No. 75-9637.

Blauner, R. 1972. *Racial Oppression in America*. New York: Harper and Row.

Blos, P. 1962. *On Adolescence: A Psychoanalytic Interpretation*. New York: The Free Press.

Bogle, D. 1989. *Toms, Coons, Mulattoes, Mammies and Bucks: An Interpretive History of Blacks in American Films*. Rev. ed. New York: Continuum.

Bradshaw, C. 1992. "Beauty and the Beast: On Racial Ambiguity." In *Racially Mixed People in America*, edited by M. Root. Newbury Park, CA: Sage Publications.

Brody, E. 1963. "Color and Identity Conflict in Young Boys." *Psychiatry* 26: 188–201.

Brown, S. 1933. "Negro Characters as Seen by White Authors." *Journal of Negro Education* 2: 194.

Brown, U. 1991. "A Study of Racial Identity, Conflict, Self-Esteem and Experiential-Physical Factors in Young Adults With One Black and One White Parent." Ph.D. diss., New York University.

———. 1995. "Black/White Interracial Young Adults: Quest for a Racial Identity." *American Journal of Orthopsychiatry* 65, no. 1: 125–130.

———. 1997. "Between Two Worlds: Psychosocial Issues of Black/White Interracial Young Adults in the USA." In *Leading Issues in African American Studies*, edited by Nikongo Ba Nikongo. Durham: Carolina Academic Press.

Brues, A. 1977. *People and Races*. New York: Macmillan.

Calhoun, A. W. 1917. *A Social History of the American Family*. Cleveland: Arthur Clark.

Carlier, A. 1867. *Marriage in the United States*. Boston: DeVries, Ibana.

Chang, T. S. (1974). "The Self-Concept of Children of Ethnically Different Marriages." *California Journal of Education Research* 25:245–252.

Cirlot, J. E. 1971. *A Dictionary of Symbols*. New York: Philosophical Library.

Clark, K., and M. Clark. 1939. "The Development of Consciousness of Self in the Emergence of Racial Identification in Negro Preschool Children." *Journal of Social Psychology* 10:591–597.

———. 1947. "Racial Identification and Racial Preference in Negro Children." In *Readings in social psychology*, edited by J. M. Newcomb and E. L. Hartley. New York: Holt.

Coates, Ta-Nehisi. 1997. "Love Knows Colors: Playing Favorites. Why Black Men Should Stick to their Own." *Washington City Paper*, 21 November.

Cooper, R. and David, R. (1986). "The Biological Concept of Race and Its Application to Public Health and Epidemiology." *Journal of Health Politics, Policy and Law* 11:99–116.

Coopersmith, Stanley (1987). *Coopersmith Self-Esteem Inventories Manual*. Palo Alto: Consulting Psychologist Press, Inc.

Cosby, C. 1998. "America Taught My Son's Killer to Hate African-Americans." *USA Today*, 8 July, 15A.

Crohn, J. 1995. *Mixed Matches: How to Create Successful Interracial, Interethnic and Interfaith Marriages*. New York: Fawcett Columbine.

Cross, W. E. 1971. "The Negro-to-Black Conversion Experience: Towards a Psychology of Black Liberation." *Black World* 29(9) p. 13–27.

Danzy, S. (1998). "The Mulatto Millennium." In *Half and half,* Claudine Chiawei O'Hare. New York: Phantom Books.

Davenport, C. B. 1917. "The Effects of Race Intermingling." *Proceedings of the American Philosophical Society* 56:364–368.

Davis, J. 1991. *Who Is Black: One Nation's Definition.* University Park: Pennsylvania State University Press.

Davis, K. 1941. "Intermarriage in Caste Societies." *American Anthropologist* 43 (July–September): 388–395.

Dearborn, M. V. 1986. *Pocahontas' Daughters.* New York: Oxford University Press.

Degler, C. N. 1986. *Neither Black Nor White: Slavery and Race Relations in Brazil and the United States.* New York: Macmillan Reprint, 1971. Madison, Wis.

Diamond, R., and R. Cottrol. 1983. "Codifying Caste: Louisiana's Racial Classification Scheme and the Fourteenth Amendment." *Loyola Law Review* 29, no. 2 (spring): 255–285.

Dien, D. S. and Vinacke, W. E., 1964. "Self-Concept and Parental Identification of Young Adults with Mixed Caucasian-Japanese Parentage." *Journal of Abnormal Psychology* 69:463–466

Drake, S. C., and H. R. Cayton. 1945. *Black Metropolis.* New York: Harcourt Brace.

Elfenbein, A. S. 1989. *Women and the Color Line: Evolving Stereotypes and the Writings of George Washington Cable, Grace King, Kate Chopin.* Charlottesville, Va.: University Press of Virginia.

Ellison, R. 1952. *The Invisible Man.* New York: Signet Classics, Mentor and Plume Books.

Erikson, E. H. 1959. "Identity and the Life Cycle." *Psychological Issues,* 1: 18–164.

———. 1963. *Childhood and Society.* 2d ed. New York: Norton.

———. 1963. *Youth: Change and Challenge.* New York: Basic Books.

———. 1968. *Identity Youth and Crisis.* New York: Norton.

Fish, J. 1996. *Culture and Therapy.* Northvale, N. J.: Jason Aronson.

Fisher, W., III. 1993. "Ideology and Imagery in the Law and Slavery" 68. Chicago Kent Law Review, p. 1051.

Fleming, R. M. 1930. "Human Hybrids." *Eugenic Review* 21:257–263.

Franklin, J. H. 1980. *From Slavery to Freedom: A History of Negro Americans.* 5th ed. New York: Alfred A. Knopf.

Frazier, F. E. 1962. *The Black Bourgeois.* New York: Collier.

———. 1957. *The Negro in the United States.* New York: Alfred A. Knopf.

Funderburg, L. 1994. *Black, White, Other: Bi-Racial Americans Talk About Racial Identity.* New York: Morrow and Company.

Gibbs, T. J. 1987. "Identity and Marginality—Issues in the Treatment of Bi-Racial Adolescents." *American Journal of Orthopsychiatry* 57:265–278.

Golden, J. 1954. "Patterns of Negro-White Intermarriage." *American Sociological Review* 19, (April): 144–166.

Gopaul-McNicol, S. 1986. "Cross-Cultural Study of the Effect of Modeling Reinforcement and Color Meaning Word Association of Black and White

Preschool Children in New York and Trinidad." Ph.D. Dissertation. Hofstra University.

Greenwald, H., and D. Oppenheimer. 1968. "Reported Magnitude of Self-identification Among Negro Children—Artifact?" *Journal Personality and Social Psychology* 16:49–52.

Grier, W., and P. Cobbs. 1968. *Black Rage*. New York: Basic Books.

Harrell S. P. 2000. "A Multidimensional Conceptualization of Racism—Related Stress: Implication for the Well-Being of People of Color." *American Journal of Orthopsychiatry* 70, no. 1: 42–57.

Hawkins, D. 1997. "The Role of Shame and Idealization in Homosexual Identity Formation." Paper presented to the U.S. Psychiatric and Mental Health Congress. 14 November, at Orlando.

Heer, D. M. 1974. "Prevalence of Black-White Marriage in the United States, 1960–1970." *Journal of Marriage and the Family* 36:246–258.

Hernton, C. 1965. *Sex and Racism in America*. Garden City: Doubleday and Company.

Holmes, S. 1996. "Census Tests New Category to Identify Racial Groups." *New York Times*, 6 December, A25.

———. 1997. "People Can Claim One or More Races on Federal Forms." *New York Times*, 30 October, 1, A26.

Holmes, S. New Policy on Census Says Those Listed as White and Minority will be Counted as Minority. *New York Times*, March 11, 2000, A9.

Hraba, J., and G. Grant. 1970. "Black Is Beautiful: A Reexamination of Racial Preference and Identification." *Journal of Personality and Social Psychology* 16:378–402.

Huggins, N. 1990. *Black Odyssey: The African-American Ordeal in Slavery*. New York: Vintage Books.

Jacobs, J. H. 1977. "Black/White Interracial Families: Marital Process, Identity and Development in Young Children." Ph.D. diss., Wright Institute.

Javier R. A., W. G. Herron, and P. T. Yanos. 1998. "Urban Poverty, Ethnicity and Personality Development." In *Personality Development and Psychotherapy in our Diverse Society*, edited by R. A. Javier and W. G. Herron. Northdale, N.J.: Jason Aronson, Inc.

Johnson, R. C., and C. T. Nagoshi. 1986. "The Adjustment of Offsprings of Within-Group and Interracial/Intercultural Marriages: A Comparison of Personality Factor Scores." *Journal of Marriage and the Family*, 48:279–284.

Kardiner, A., and Ovesey, L. 1962. *The Mark of Oppression*. Cleveland: World Publishing Co.

King, J. 1981. *The Biology of Race*. Berkeley: University of California Press.

Krauss, W. W. 1941. Race Crossing in Hawaii. *Journal of Heredity* 32:371–378.

Ladner, J. 1984. Providing a Healthy Environment for Interracial Children. *Interracial Books for Children Bulletin* 15, no. 6:7–8.

Lebsock, S. 1990. "No Obey." In *Women, Families and Communities: Readings in American History*. Vol. 1, to 1877, edited by N. Hewitt. Glenview, Ill.: Foresman/Little.

Little, G. (1942). "Analytic Reflection of Mixed Marriages." *Psychoanalytic Review* 29: 20–25.

Lofgren, C. A. 1987. *The Plessey Case*. New York: Oxford University Press.

Lombardo, P. 1988. "Miscegenation, Eugenics and Racism: Historical Footnotes to Lovings vs. Virginia." *M. C. Davis Law Review* 21, no. 2 (winter 1988), 421–452.

Lythcott-Haimes, J. 1994. "Where Do Mixed Babies Belong? Racial Classification in America and Its Implication for Transracial Adoption." *Harvard Civil Rights Civil Liberty Law Review* 29, no. 2 (summer): 529–558.

Marriot, M. 1996. Multiracial Americans Ready to Claim Their Own Identity. *New York Times*, 20 July, 1.

Martelle, D. 1970. "Interracial Marriage Attitudes Among High School Students." *Psychological Reports* 27:1007–1010.

McAdoo, H. 1985. "Racial Attitudes and Self-Concept of Young Black Children Over Time." In *Black Children: Social, Educational and Parental Environments*, edited by H. McAdoo, and J. McAdoo. Beverly Hills: Sage Publications.

McLean, H. 1963. "The Emotional Health of Negroes." In *Mental Health and Segregation*, edited by M. Grossack. New York: Springer.

Merton, R. 1941. "Intermarriage and the Social Structure: Fact and Theory." *Psychiatry*, 4: 361–374.

Mills, C. 1998. Interrace Online. A Service to Interrace Magazine.

Monahan, T. P. 1976. "The Occupational Class of Couples Entering into Interracial Marriages." *Journal of Comparative Family Studies* Vol VII, no. 2 (summer): 175–192.

Money-Kyrle R. 1960. "On Prejudice—A Psychoanalytic Approach." *British Journal of Medical Psychology* 33:205–209.

Montague, F., and A. Montague. 1940. "Problems and Methods to the Study of Race." *Psychiatry* III, no. 4:493–506.

Moore, B. E., and B. D. Fine, eds. 1991. *Psychoanalytic Terms and Concepts*. New Haven, Conn.: Yale University Press.

Moreland, K. 1966. "A Comparison of Race Awareness in Northern and Southern Children." *American Orthopsychiatry Association* 36: 22–31.

Morrison, T. 1970. *The Bluest Eye*. New York: Holt.

Moskovitz, M. 1998. "Blackness, Ethnicity and the Fantasy of Ethnicity." In *Personality Development and Psychotherapy in Our Diverse Society*, edited by R. Javier and W. Herron. Northdale, N.J.: Jason Aronson, Inc.

Murstein, B. 1973. "A Theory of Marital Choice Applied to Interracial Marriage." In *Interracial Marriage: Expectations and Realities*, edited by I. Stuart and L. E. Abt. New York: Grossman Publishers.

Myers, H. F., and L. M. King. 1983. "Mental Health Issues in the Development of the Black American Child." In *The Psycho-Social Development of Minority Group Children*, edited by G. J. Powell. New York: Brunner/Mazel.

Myrdal, G. 1944. *An American Dilemma*. New York: Harper and Row.

Nakashima, L. L. 1992. "An Invisible Monster. The Creation and Denial of Mixed Race People in America." In *Racially Mixed People in America*, edited by M. Root. Newbury Park, CA: Sage Publications.

Nevid J., and R. Goodman. 1998. "Race, Ethnicity and Mental Illness." In *Personality Development and Psychotherapy in Our Diverse Society*, edited by R. Javier and W. Herron. Northdale, N.J.: Jason Aronson, Inc.

Newton, R. K. 1941. "Intermarriage and the Social Structure: Fact and Theory." *Psychiatry* 4:361–374.

Njeri, I. 1993. "Sushi and Grits." In *Lure and Loathing*, edited by G. Early. New York: Penguin Books.

Office of Management and Budget. 1999. *Draft Provisional Guidance on the Implementation of the 1997 Standards for the Collection of Federal Data on Race and Ethnicity*. Washington D.C. 17 February.

O'Hearne, Claudine Chiawei (1998). *Half and Half*. New York: Pantheon Books.

Park, R. E. 1928. "Human Migration and the Marginal Man." *American Journal of Sociology* 33:881–893.

Park, R. E. 1931. "Mentality of Racial Hybrids." *American Journal of Sociology*, 36: 534–551.

Parker, J. 1971. *Black Child, White Child*. Cambridge: Harvard University Press.

Payne, R. B. 1977. "Racial Attitude Formation: Children of Mixed Black and White Heritage, Skin Color and Racial Identity." Ph.D. diss., California School of Professional Psychology.

Pederson, P. B. 1991. "Multiculturalism as a Generic Approach in Counseling." *Journal of Counseling and Development* 70, no. 1: 6–12.

Petrioni, F. 1971. "Teenage Interracial Dating." *Transaction* 8 (September): 54–59.

Petrioni, F., and E. Hirsch 1970. *Two, Four, Six, Eight. When You Gonna Integrate?* New York: Behavioral Publications.

Pettigrew, T. F. 1964. *A Profile of the American Negro*. Princeton, N.J.: Van Nostrand.

Phillips, P. (1984). *What Do Bi-Racial Children Need?* New York: *Bi-Racial Resource Center*.

Piskacek, V., and M. Golub. 1973. "Children of Interracial Marriage." In *Interracial Marriage: Expectations and Realities*, edited by I. Stuart and L. E. Abt. New York: Grossman.

Porter, J. (1971). *Black Child, White Child*. Cambridge Mass: Harvard University Press.

Porterfield, E. 1978. *Black and White Mixed Marriages*. Chicago: Nelson-Hall.

Poussaint, A. F. 1984. "A Study of Interracial Children Presents Positive Picture." *Bulletin, Interracial Books for Children* 15, no. 6:9–10.

Powell-Hopson, D. 1985. "The Effects of Modeling Reinforcement in Color Meaning Word Association on Doll Preference of Black and White Preschool Children." Ph.D. diss., Hofstra University.

Provine, W. B. 1973. Geneticists and the Biology of Race Crossing. *Science* 182: 790–796.

Reuter, E. B. 1918. *The Mulatto in the United States: Including a Study of the Role of Mixed-Blood Races throughout the World*. Boston: Badger/Gorham Press.

———. 1938. *The American Race Problem*. New York: Crowell.

———. [1931]. *Race Mixture*. New York: Negro University Press.

Ring, J. M. (2000, January). The Long and Winding Road: Personal Reflections of an Anti-Racism Trainer. *American Journal of Orthopsychiatry* 70, no. 1 (January):73–81.

Roberts, R. E. 1983. "Self-Identification and Social Status of Bi-Racial Children in Chicago in Comparative Perspective." Paper presented to the International Congress of Anthropology and Ethnological Sciences, 20 August, at Vancouver.

Root, M. 1992. *Racially Mixed People in America*. Newbury Park, CA: Sage Publications.

Rouse, D. 1997. Race Against Prejudice. Washington, D.C.: *Washington City Paper* 21 November, 34.

Russell, K., M. Wilson, and W. Hall. 1992. *The Color Complex: The Politics of Skin Color Among African-Americans*. New York: Anchor Books, Doubleday.

Sawyer K. (1998). List of National Interracial Support/Advocacy Groups. Baltimore, M.D.

Scales-Trent, J. 1995: *Notes of a White Black Woman*. University Park: Pennsylvania University Press.

Scheick, W. J. 1979. *The Half-Blood: A Cultural Symbol in 19th Century American Fiction*. Lexington: University of Kentucky Press.

Schemo, D. J. 2000. Despite Options on Census, Many to Check 'Black' Only. *New York Times*, 12 February, A1, A 10.

Sebald, H. 1968. Patterns of Interracial Dating and Sexual Liaison of White and Black College Men. *International Journal of Sociology of the Family* 4, no. 4 (Spring):23–36.

Sewell, T. E. 1985. "Review of the Coopersmith Self-Esteem Inventory." In *Mental Measurement Yearbook*, edited by J. V. Mitchell. Lincoln, Neb.: Buros Institute of Mental Measurement.

Shannon, A. H. 1930. *The Negro in Washington, A Study of Racial Amalgamation*. New York: Widle Neale.

Sickels, R. J. 1972. *Race, Marriage and the Law*. Albuquerque: University of New Mexico Press.

Smith, W. C. 1939. "The Hybrid in Hawaii as a Marginal Man." *American Journal of Sociology* 39:459–468.

Smothers, R. 1994. "Principal Causes Furor on Mixed-Race Couples." *New York Times*, 16 March, 16.

Spencer, J. M. 1997. *The New Colored People*. New York: New York University Press.

Spickard, P. 1992. "The Illogic of American Racial Categories." In *Racially Mixed People in America*, edited by M. Root. Newbury Park, CA: Sage Publication.

———. 1989. *Mixed Blood. Intermarriage and Ethnic Identity in Twentieth-Century America*. Madison: University of Wisconsin Press.

Spivey, P. 1984. "Interracial Adolescents: Self-Image, Racial Self-Concept and Family Process." Ph.D. diss., City University of New York.

———. 1984. Growing up in interracial families. *Interracial Books for Children Bulletin* 15, no. 6:11–16.

———. 1984. "Physical Characteristics Scales. In *Interracial Adolescents: Self-Image, Racial Self-Concept and Family Process*. Ph.D. diss., City University of New York.

Spurlock, J. 1986. "Development of Self-Conception in Afro-American Children." *Hospital and Community Psychiatry*, January, vol. 37, no. 1: 66–70.

Staples, R. 1968. "Negro-White Sex: Facts and Fiction." *Sexology Magazine* 35 (August): 48.

Stedman, R. 1982. *Shadows of the Indian: Stereotypes in American Culture.* Norman: University of Oklahoma Press.

Steinberg, S. 1981. *The Ethnic Myth.* Boston: Beacon.

Steinhorn L., and B. Diggs-Brown. 2000 *By the Color of Our Skin.* New York: Penguin Books.

Stepakoff, S., and L. Bowleg. 1997. "Sexual Identity in Sociocultural Context: Clinical Implications of Multiple Marginalization." In R. Javier and W. Herron. *Personality Development and Psychotherapy in Our Diverse Society*, Northdale, N.J.: Jason Aronson, Inc.

Stonequist, E. 1937. *The Marginal Man: A Study in Personality and Culture Conflict.* New York: Scribner and Sons.

Stuckard, R. 1958. "The African Ancestry of the White Population." *Ohio Journal of Science* 58:155–160.

Tatum, B. D. 1997. *Why Are All the Black Kids Sitting Together in the Cafeteria?* New York: Basic Books.

Teicher, J. 1968, March. "Some Observations of Identity Problems in Children of Negro-White Marriages." *Journal of Mental Disease* 46:249–256.

The Random House Dictionary of the English Language 1987. New York: Random House, 1261.

Thernstrom, S., and A. Thernstrom 1997. *America in Black and White: One Nation Indivisible.* New York: Simon and Schuster, Touchstone Book.

Thurman, W. 1970. *The Blacker the Berry.* London: Macaulay, 1929. Reprint, New York: Macmillan.

United States Bureau of the Census 1994. "Household and Family Characteristics." *Current Population Reports*, Series P 20–48. March. Washington, D.C.: Author.

United States Bureau of the Census 1998. *Current Population Reports.* Marital Series P 20–514. March. Washington, D.C.

Ward, S. H. and Braun, J. (1972). "Status and Living Arrangements." "Self-Esteem and Racial Preference in Black Children." *Journal of American Orthopsychiatry* 42 (4), 644–647.

Warner, J. 1987. "Clinical Practice With Bi-Racial Families." Paper presented at the Annual Conference of the American Orthopsychiatry Association, April 19, 1987, Washington, D.C.

Washington City Paper 1997. Quoting without Citation the Results of a Gallup Poll published in *U.S.A. Today*, 21 November.

Washington, J. 1970. *Marriage in Black and White.* Boston: Beacon Press.

Williams, Ch. R. 1981. "Adaptation of the Black-White Mixed Child." Ph.D. diss., University of Northern Colorado.

Williamson, J. 1980. *New People: Miscegenation and Mulattoes in the United States.* New York: Free Press.

Willie, C., and J. Levy. 1972. Black Is Lonely. *Psychology Today* 5 (March): 50–52.

White-Stephan, C. 1992. "Mixed-Heritage Individuals: Ethnic Identity and Trait Characteristics." In *Racially Mixed People in America*, edited by M. Root. Newbury Park, CA. Sage Publications.

Wrenn, C. G. 1962. "The Culturally-Encapsulated Counselor." *Harvard Educational Review* 32:444–49.

Yankelovich Partners, Inc., 1996. "African-American Study: Topline Report," prepared for the *New Yorker*, March, 29.

Index

About the Author

URSULA M. BROWN is a psychotherapist in private practice in Montclair, New Jersey. Among Dr. Brown's areas of concentration are the treatment of interracial, cross-cultural, and interreligious families. Her articles have appeared in various journals, including *American Journal of Orthopsychiatry.*